CITY EATS

NEW ORLEANS

50+ RECIPES FROM THE BEST OF THE BIG EASY

BETH D'ADDONO

CIDER MILL
PRESS

BOOK
PUBLISHERS

CITY EATS: NEW ORLEANS

13-Digit ISBN: 978-1-40034-068-2
10-Digit ISBN: 1-40034-068-3

This book may be ordered by mail from the publisher. Please include $5.99 for postage and handling. Please support your local bookseller first!

Books published by Cider Mill Press Book Publishers are available at special discounts for bulk purchases in the United States by corporations, institutions, and other organizations. For more information, please contact the publisher.

Cider Mill Press Book Publishers
"Where good books are ready for press"
501 Nelson Place
Nashville, Tennessee 37214

cidermillpress.com

Typography: FreightSans Pro, FreightText Pro,
P22 Arts and Crafts Hunter, Sackers Gothic Std

Printed in Malaysia

24 25 26 27 28 COS 5 4 3 2 1

First Edition

TOUPS' MEATERY

845 N. CARROLLTON TEL : 504.252.4999

MEATERY ⚜ MIDCITY NOLA ⚜

TOUPSMEATERY.COM

CARRY OUT & DELIVERY (DELIVERY 5-9 ONLY)

Toup's Meatery
See page 264

CONTENTS

Commander's Palace Restaurant

See page 37

INTRODUCTION

WHAT NEW ORLEANS EATS AND WHY: AN EVOLVING NARRATIVE

Much has been written about how New Orleans restaurants survived, shifted, and managed to thrive after Katrina essentially eradicated the city's hospitality scene. Despite the challenges of opening during the long period of recovery, new restaurants managed to do just that. Some chefs left, but many came back, energized by new experiences and interesting ideas.

But when the global pandemic shuttered restaurants worldwide in March 2020, local chefs couldn't get a job in Houston or New York to wait out the storm. There was nowhere to go. Everything changed overnight. How the restaurant scene has weathered this unprecedented event speaks volumes to the strength and resilience of the New Orleans hospitality community.

Prior to the stay-at-home mandate issued on March 20 by the mayor's office, I'd been reviewing restaurants weekly for *Gambit*, one of my regular freelance outlets. As everything ground to a halt, anxiety and fear replaced the usual joie de vivre that draws so many people to visit and even move to New Orleans. Everybody was out of work overnight. At a time when we'd normally turn to friends and family for solace and shoring up, our communities contracted into miniscule pods. Dining out as we knew it was over, for who knew how long. There were no restaurants to review.

Then something amazing happened. It was August, with the pandemic full-on raging. A vaccine was on the horizon, but still four months away. One of my editors, Will Coviello at *Gambit*, called me and said he'd noticed something surprising. New restaurants were opening, in a climate of social distancing, mask mandates, and high anxiety. Some of these were projects long in the works. Others the result of a "what the hell, if not now, when?" sensibility. "We should be covering this," he said. So, I did.

I've written about one new restaurant a week since then, more than two hundred stories about dreams and plans, seemingly insurmountable challenges, and the grit it takes to survive endless pivots. Half of the restaurants mentioned in *City Eats: New Orleans* weren't around before 2020. Stitched together with the existing hospitality community, a new culinary narrative is unfolding. As important as the Creole influence is on New Orleans cuisine, it is not the only story to tell. At its best, the New Orleans dining scene reflects the city's diverse history and culture. It's a conversation that continues to evolve.

CREOLE FLAVORS, AND BEYOND

As a baseline, New Orleans is a town of rabid eaters who start talking about what they're going to have for dinner before lunch is over. Crackling with an effusive culinary history and cocktail culture, New Orleans is arguably the best place to eat in America. Just ask anybody who lives here.

New Orleans has long been defined by the evolution of Creole cuisine, a style of cooking that is absolutely a sum of its parts. It started with recipes brought by French settlers, but soon grew to include herbs and filé, or ground sassafras leaves, used by locally indigenous people, including the Choctaw tribe. Saffron and peppers were introduced by the Spanish. Enslaved Africans brought new ingredients as well as cooking acumen and techniques with them on their forced diaspora. From the West Indies came different fruits and vegetables, spices, and sugarcane. Then, the tidal wave of Sicilian immigration in the late nineteenth century added even more ingredients and methods to the mix.

Cajun cooks expanded the lexicon, bringing rustic French country cooking based on farm-, Gulf-, and swamp-to-table ingredients into their versions of smothered, sautéed, smoked, and grilled dishes. The late great chef Paul Prudhomme revolutionized both Cajun and Creole cuisine, bringing dishes like blackened redfish forever into the mainstream.

And the city's palate continued to expand. Vietnamese cuisine was brought by a wave of immigrants in the 1970s and is now forever linked to what locals crave, from pho to Viet Cajun seafood boils. Same for Mexican and Central American cuisine, introduced by many of the workers and their families who came to help rebuild the city after Katrina. A New Orleans without pupuserías and taquerias is now unthinkable.

While the French Quarter is home to so many important restaurants, neighborhood pride influences dining all over town. Uptown are places like St. James Cheese Company, Costera for authentic Spanish cuisine, and Casamento's Restaurant for oysters. Gris-Gris and Lengua Madre enliven the Garden District. Miss Shirley's Chinese Restaurant and Joey K's shake things up in the Irish Channel. Emeril's and Carmo offer dynamic options in the Warehouse Arts District; Dooky Chase's Restaurant in Tremé; and Katie's, Marjie's Grill, and Crescent City Steaks in Mid-City. The Central Business District (CBD) is alive with notable restaurants, places like chef Michael Gulotta's Maypop, chef Nina Compton's Caribbean-influenced Compère Lapin, and the coastal French fare of King.

The late New Orleans restaurant matriarch Miss Ella Brennan famously said that whereas in other places, one eats to live, "in New Orleans, we live to eat." That big appetite will never be satisfied.

#EQUITYINHOSPITALITY

During the 2023 New Orleans Entrepreneur Week, produced by the entrepreneur-focused nonprofit The Idea Village, equity in hospitality was much discussed. One of the many panels was "Unprecedented Possibility: Laying the Foundation for the Future for the Owner/Chef/Entrepreneur in New Orleans and Beyond."

Moderated by Lauren Darnell, the executive director of the Made in New Orleans Foundation (MiNO), the discussion centered on how the hospitality industry has had to reinvent itself, bear the threat and risk to health, cultivate adaptability, navigate uncertainty, and remain open, all the while feeding the city. The conversation was led by a panel of BIPOC chefs and committed restaurateurs, change makers who are helping to transform hospitality in New Orleans for the better.

Like most other cities in the United States, the restaurant industry here has historically been dominated by white-owned businesses. Giving voice to the BIPOC hospitality community and culture bearers that bring millions of visitors to the city every year is at the heart of this conversation.

While much work is still left to be done to address systemic inequalities, many dedicated people and organizations are working to support and uplift BIPOC-owned restaurants in the city.

Organizations like MiNO work to grow, support, and finance the success of BIPOC hospitality professionals. Turning Tables is another change maker, striving to create a foundation for equity, diversity, leadership, and career pathways in the bartending and hospitality community.

Nationally renowned bartender Abigail Gullo, creative director at Loa Bar in the International House Hotel, sees a lot of progress when it comes to bringing more women and people of color into the conversation. "There's been movement, thanks to organizations like Turning Tables, but they can only do so much," she said. "The real work has to be done in the community."

Change is happening today in the New Orleans restaurant community. There is a growing heterogenous vision of what we eat and why we eat it. The table has expanded to include more kinds of cuisine, including flavors rooted in African, Black American, and Caribbean culture, long marginalized.

Women are in more positions of leadership, helping to create equity and diversity steeped in respect and kindness.

While much more work is yet to be done, the hospitality for which New Orleans has long been known is deeply entrenched in our DNA. Things are going in the right direction. Most importantly, New Orleans is here to stay. As we look to the future, there is reason for hope.

Note: At the time of writing this book, all of the featured restaurants were open and thriving. It's the nature of the industry that closures happen. We still recognize the hardworking chefs behind places that have closed, or are continuing to evolve.

HERBSAINT
See page 164

GUIDE TO FEATURED RESTAURANTS BY NEIGHBORHOOD

The restaurants in this book represent New Orleans food cultures, and to let each establishment be represented as a singular part of a unified whole, we have organized them alphabetically. But if you are looking for a spot in a specific neighborhood, look no further.

BAYOU ST. JOHN/ MID-CITY

Addis NOLA
Queen Trini Lisa Island Soul Food
Rosedale
Toups' Meatery

BYWATER/ MARIGNY

Alma Café
Black Roux Culinary Collective
Bywater Bakery
The Elysian Bar

CENTRAL CITY

Café Reconcile
Deelightful Roux School of Cooking

CENTRAL BUSINESS DISTRICT/CBD

Compère Lapin at the Old No. 77
Copper Vine
Couvant
Miss River
Chemin à la Mer

Johnny Sánchez
Maypop

COVINGTON/ NORTHSHORE

Del Porto Ristorante

FRENCH QUARTER

Arnaud's
Café Sbisa
Cane & Table
GW Fins
MaMou
Saint John
Tujague's

GRETNA/ ALGIERS POINT

Thai D-Jing
Tonti's French Bistro

METAIRIE

Banh Mi Boys

LOWER GARDEN DISTRICT/ GARDEN DISTRICT

Commander's Palace
Gris-Gris

Jack Rose
Le Chat Noir
Lengua Madre
San Lorenzo
The Bower
Turkey and the Wolf
Union Ramen

TREME/SEVENTH WARD

8 Fresh Food Assassin Restaurant & Lounge
Fritai

UPTOWN

Dakar NOLA
LUVI
Mister Mao
Mucho Más
Saba
Seafood Sally's
The Chloe

WAREHOUSE ARTS DISTRICT

Emeril's
Herbsaint

Turkey and the Wolf
See page 280

ADDIS NOLA

2514 Bayou Road
addisnola.com

BRINGS THE FLAVORS OF ETHIOPIA TO NEW ORLEANS

Addis NOLA began, like so many of life's wonders, with one woman's brilliant idea. Although she came to the city to teach public policy at Southern University at New Orleans, Dr. Biruk Alemayehu found herself thinking a lot about the dearth of Ethiopian cuisine in the city.

"I wanted to share my country's cuisine with New Orleans. I just had to get my family on board."

A native of Ethiopia, she and her husband, Jaime Lobo, immigrated to the United States to go to school at LSU in Baton Rouge. Lobo, who hails from Angola in Central Africa, studied veterinary medicine and is a mosquito virologist. The family moved with their young son, Prince, to New Orleans in 2009.

"It was my vision," recalled Biruk. "I came up with this crazy idea, with no experience in the restaurant business. And my family immediately supported me." With the help of experienced Ethiopian restaurateur and chef Sammy Shifferaw, Addis NOLA opened its doors in 2019 at the busy corner of Tulane Avenue and Broad Street. In 2022, with Jaime leading the kitchen, Addis moved to a larger location on Bayou Road, a historic hub for Black-owned businesses and New Orleans's oldest road.

Ethiopian fare builds on a foundation of slow cooking and layered spices. Deeply flavored iconic stews and braised dishes simmer with caramelized onions and garlic in a blend of robust spices. Wot is Ethiopia's national dish, an earthy, thick stew served on top of injera, a fermented pancake-like, stretchy flatbread that takes almost three days to make. Tradition is to eat it by hand, tearing off bits of bread and scooping up a dish like shrimp wot, made with large Gulf shrimp, or rib eye tibs, a stir-fry of steak with onions, tomatoes, jalapeños, fresh herbs, and butter.

Vegetarians can tuck into all of the favorites prepared meatless, including mushroom tibs, sweet potato wot, spiced red lentils, collards, beets, and cabbage with carrots—all savory options.

With a flavor profile that balances spicy with sour and pungent tastes, many Ethiopian dishes incorporate berbere, a blend of up to sixteen spices, from cumin to coriander and cardamom. It's important to the the Alemayehu and Lobo family that their guests understand the origins of a dish and how it relates to Ethiopian culture.

Although it might take a minute to get used to picking up the bits of meat and veg with strips of spongy injera, the best way to experience Ethiopian cuisine is to lean into the communal dining experience, which brings warm hospitality to the table.

DORO WOT

Addis NOLA co-owner Dr. Biruk Alemayehu remembers the excitement she felt as a little girl, the anticipation that came with peeling what seemed like five hundred onions for Doro Wot, a special dish reserved for occasions like Christmas, New Year's, and Easter. The time and love invested in this one stew led to a celebratory meal with special guests, friends, and family enjoying the vibrant essence of this dish. A central ingredient of Doro Wot is berbere, a fiery, bright-red, and flavorful Ethiopian spice blend made fresh with whole spices. For the home cook, there are excellent premade blends for sale at gourmet stores and online spice markets. Although traditionally stewed for twelve hours, the dish comes together fine in four, mostly unattended. It's best enjoyed scooped up with gluten-free injera or another neutral bread, to let the stew's flavor dominate.

SERVES 6-8

1 WHOLE CHICKEN, CUT INTO PIECES

3 TABLESPOONS FRESH LEMON JUICE OR WHITE VINEGAR

3 POUNDS RED ONIONS, PEELED

2 TABLESPOONS VEGETABLE OIL

3 TABLESPOONS FINELY MINCED GARLIC

2 TABLESPOONS FINELY MINCED GINGER

1–2 CUPS BERBERE

7 CUPS WATER

12 EGGS, HARD-BOILED AND PEELED

3 TABLESPOONS UNSALTED BUTTER

1. Put chicken in bowl; add lemon juice or vinegar and stir to coat. Set aside.

2. Cut red onions into quarters and add to food processor. Pulse a few times, scraping down sides until you have a chunky puree.

continued...

3. Add oil to 3- or 4-quart heavy saucepan, preferably a cast-iron Dutch oven, set over medium-low heat. Add red onion puree and cook over low heat at least 2 hours.

4. Add garlic and ginger to pot. Simmer on low an additional 30 minutes to 1 hour to blend flavors.

5. Add berbere and let mixture simmer another 1 hour until thickened.

6. After berbere and onions reduce to a dark, thick sauce called kulet, add chicken and half the water. Cook 30 minutes and then add remaining water, cooking another 30 minutes to 1 hour until chicken is tender. If you like your stew thicker, add less water, or if you prefer more sauce, add more water.

7. Poke holes into boiled eggs with fork to help infuse flavor, and add to stew. Stir in butter. Remove from heat and let stew rest at least 30 minutes to let flavors mingle before serving.

ALMA CAFÉ

800 Louisa Street
eatalmanola.com

A CHEF REMEMBERS HER GRANDMOTHER

For chef Melissa Araujo, the modern Honduran food she makes at Alma Café is personal. Araujo was born in La Ceiba, on the Atlantic coast of Honduras, the ninth daughter of a Sicilian mother and a Honduran-Portuguese father. Her parents' photo hangs in her Bywater restaurant. As far back as she can remember, the family table was the heart of her home.

She grew up in Providence, Rhode Island, and moved to New Orleans at sixteen, but her summers were spent in Honduras on her grandmother's farm, cooking and working by her side, an early immersion in fresh, local, seasonal ingredients that continues to inform and influence her culinary philosophy. Although she tried to study law, her father's wish, Melissa's passion was always food. "I did not choose this profession. The profession picked me," said the chef.

Melissa started working in restaurants and cooked for six years in Italy before coming back to New Orleans kitchens, including Doris Metropolitan and Restaurant R'evolution. After running Alma for five years as a pop-up, she opened the restaurant in homage to her grandmother's kitchen in the fall of 2020. The name means "soul" in Spanish, something she feels at her essence. A black-and-white tile depiction of the Mayan moon goddess Ix Chel, a deity of female power and fertility, also speaks to her strength as a queer woman with big ideas and ambition.

The fifty-five-seat restaurant was busy from day one, serving breakfast, brunch, and lunch. Although there a growing number of casual mom-and-pop Honduran restaurants around town, at Alma, the chef takes modern Honduran flavors to the next level.

Her baleadas sencilla are legend, a staple of the restaurant's morning business from the start. Simply addictive, a crispy folded-over flour tortilla arrives filled with mashed refried beans, homemade crema, and salty queso duro. Add chorizo, marinated pork, brisket, or mushrooms as you like. Other popular breakfast options are a fried chicken thigh topped with sage-and-chorizo gravy, and an egg and crawfish tails with a cathead biscuit on the side.

The lunch menu offers chicharrones and cracklins served with disks of fried green plantains and pickled onions. Although pork-belly salad sounds like a misnomer, this dish offers a contrast of textures and flavors, with crisp layers of meat, fresh herbs, and salad greens dressed in a coconut-milk vinaigrette.

The chef continues to grow her business, most recently opening Oscar, a café for sophisticated bar food inside Pirogue's Whiskey Bayou, a tavern three miles from Alma in Chalmette. It's another sign that she's here to stay, rooted in New Orleans. Melissa recently bought her first home in Chalmette, a space for kin and friends to gather around her own family table.

Baleadas Sencilla
See page 28

BALEADAS SENCILLA

Considered the national dish of Honduras, baleadas originated along the northern coast but are now sold as comfort food in every corner of the country. Thick, soft flour tortillas are folded over a variety of fillings. Baleadas sencilla is the dish at its most basic, filled with refried beans, Honduran crema, and queso seco, a dry cheese available at Latin grocery stores. For the tortillas, chef Melissa advises adjusting the amount of water depending on how warm your hands are naturally. Or just follow the recipe.

SERVES 6-8

TORTILLAS

3 CUPS ALL-PURPOSE FLOUR

2½ TEASPOONS BAKING SODA

1 TEASPOON KOSHER SALT

1 EGG

1 CUP WARM WATER

¼ CUP LARD, UNSALTED BUTTER, OR OIL, ROOM TEMPERATURE

1. In large bowl, mix flour, baking soda, salt, egg, warm water, and lard, mixing by hand to a soft, sticky, uniform dough.

2. Let rest 15–20 minutes so dough will be easier to work with.

3. Make 6-8 dough balls and let rest 15–20 minutes more.

4. Using rolling pin, stretch out dough into shape of a round tortilla. True experts can make a final touch with their hands, but it requires some practice.

5. Cook tortillas on hot pan 2 minutes or until brown on both sides. Stack tortillas; they will steam and stay soft and warm for a longer time.

BALEADAS

1 16-OUNCE CAN REFRIED BEANS

1 TEASPOON SALT

HOT SAUCE, TO TASTE (OPTIONAL)

2 CUPS HONDURAN QUESO SECO
OR COTIJA CHEESE

½ CUP HONDURAN CREMA

1 AVOCADO, SLICED (OPTIONAL)

½ CUP CILANTRO, CHOPPED
(OPTIONAL)

½ CUP CRUMBLED FRIED CHORIZO
(OPTIONAL)

1. Warm beans in small skillet, adding salt and hot sauce, if using.

2. For each baleada, spread about ¼ cup beans, ¼ cup cheese, and 1 tablespoon Honduran crema on a tortilla. Top with any other desired fillings. Fold in half and enjoy a classic baleada.

ARNAUD'S

813 Bienville Street
arnaudsrestaurant.com

ARNAUD'S HONORS TRADITION ON THE PLATE

Besides God and country, generations of New Orleanians have long pledged their allegiance to their favorite old-school Creole restaurant. Oftentimes the choice is something they've inherited, like the hulking armoire from their maternal grandmother that commands center stage in the master bedroom. Other times fierce loyalty is inspired firsthand, a relationship informed by personal connection and hours of tending to from servers who have taken care of guests for decades.

Katy Casbarian understands that innate sense of loyalty. As co-owner of Arnaud's restaurant, the largest of the city's fine Creole palaces, she entertains a cavalcade of regulars, and she's thankful for that. But therein also lies a challenge.

"We are always trying to reach out to locals and get them in the door, to see us with a fresh eye. Staying relevant is always part of our conversation."

Chef de cuisine Tommy DiGiovanni, in Arnaud's kitchen for more than two decades, delivers menu classics with unwavering consistency while introducing creative dishes like breast of duck Ellen served with marinated blueberries and a blueberry-infused port wine sauce. A spiced café brûlot powered by orange curaçao and flamed with brandy is a signature way to end an Arnaud's feast.

If the entire restaurant and all fourteen private dining rooms are full, 950 guests will be expecting the likes of oysters Bienville, trout meunière, shrimp Arnaud, and crab cakes topped with the chef's proprietary mustard-forward rémoulade sauce.

Arnaud's comes by its French Quarter pedigree honestly. The restaurant turned 105 in 2023, having been founded in 1918 by French wine salesman Arnaud Cazenave. Two families have been owners, the Cazenaves and now the Casbarians, in their second generation of leadership with Katy and her brother, Archie, managing since their father's untimely death in 2009. Taking up close to a city block just off Bourbon Street on Bienville, Arnaud's is striking without being showy. The tiled main dining room is legendary, with its glowing chandeliers, flickering candlelight, and tall leaded-glass windows. Then there's the James Beard Award–winning French 75 Bar and the Jazz Bistro, an intimate dining room with a jazz brunch on Sundays.

According to Katy, the trick is to tread lightly in a place steeped in history, keeping one foot in the past, with another firmly planted in the future.

"Part of the restaurant's success comes from staying true to its roots and not deviating too much," she said. "We'd have a revolt if we made too many changes. At the same time, chef Tommy offers lighter options, like a simply grilled local pompano with lemon and herbs. We are committed to showing reverence for the past and respect for our history, which will always be at the core of who we are."

ARNAUD'S, FRENCH QUARTER

French wine merchant Arnaud Cazenave opened the grand restaurant bearing his name in 1918. The restaurant's been in the Casbarian family since 1978, with the fourth generation, Archie and his sister, Katy, now at the helm. The wine cellar is legendary.

Signature dish: Shrimp Arnaud

BRENNAN'S, FRENCH QUARTER

A beacon of pink on Royal Street since 1946, Brennan's is renowned for serving "breakfast," a groaning repast that involves brandy milk punch, signature eggs Hussarde, and bananas Foster, a flaming wow that first impressed here.

Signature dish: Bananas Foster

BROUSSARD'S, FRENCH QUARTER

Broussard's has celebrated milestones with locals since 1920. Chef Jimi Setchim presents a modern Creole menu with lighter sauces and garnishes and a nod to the flavors of the Caribbean. The restaurant's stunning courtyard is ideal for glittering parties.

Signature dish: Bronzed redfish with crabmeat and lemon beurre blanc

COMMANDER'S PALACE, FRENCH QUARTER

Commanding the table since 1893, this romantic Victorian mansion prides itself on exquisite service and classy Creole cooking. Most ingredients are sourced locally. Chef Meg Bickford is the first woman to lead the Commander's Palace kitchen, which has seen chefs from Paul Prudhomme to Emeril Lagasse in that role. Sunday offers a lively jazz brunch.

Signature dish: Bread pudding soufflé

GALATOIRE'S, FRENCH QUARTER

Friday lunch has been a tradition at Galatoire's on Bourbon Street for generations, since 1905. It's a party notable for high fashion, flowing champagne, and decadent excess. Some of the best waiters in the city serve platters of trout meunière, shrimp rémoulade, and stuffed eggplant.

Signature dish: Turtle soup

NEW(ER) KIDS ON THE CREOLE BLOCK

These "newer" restaurants, as in less than a century old, offer an adored mix of French and Creole Italian specialties.

DICKIE BRENNAN'S BOURBON HOUSE, FRENCH QUARTER

Dickie Brennan's modern New Orleans fish house boasts one of the best oyster bars in town and an outstanding version of barbecue shrimp finished with—what else—bourbon. Classic Creole fare includes a tasty seafood-and-sausage gumbo.

Signature dish: Redfish grilled on the half shell

BRIGTSEN'S, UPTOWN

Frank Brigtsen is an iconic New Orleans gentleman chef, an inventive Creole cook who apprenticed under chef Paul Prudhomme. In 1986, he and his wife, Marna, opened Brigtsen's in 1986—a remarkable and original restaurant that continues to thrive—in a homey Victorian cottage in the Riverbend. The chef's accolades are too many to mention, but his cooking—that's the real prize.

Signature dish: Fried des Allemands catfish

CLANCY'S, UPTOWN

Tucked away in residential Uptown, this family-owned traditional Creole restaurant oozes old-style New Orleans charm. The former bar and po'boy shop has been a white-tablecloth eatery since the 1980s, a favorite of locals who want Galatoire's without going to the Quarter.

Signature dish: Fried oysters with brie

GABRIELLE RESTAURANT, MID-CITY

Chef Greg Sonnier delivers favorites like barbecued shrimp pie and peppermint patti, as well as new dishes like paneed veal with lobster ravioli and lobster brie sauce. The restaurant's trademark warmth and hospitality are a respite any day, but are especially notable for a celebration.

Signature dish: Slow-roasted duck

IRENE'S, FRENCH QUARTER

Irene's has dished memorable French and Creole Italian cooking since 1992. Lasagna Bolognese, duck St. Phillip with raspberry-pancetta demi-glace, and oysters Irene are legend.

Signature dish: Meunière amandine with lump crabmeat

MR. B'S, FRENCH QUARTER

Cindy Brennan opened this beacon of hospitality and Creole specialties in 1979. It hasn't missed a beat, with service and the satisfying menu always stellar. Gumbo ya-ya, barbecue shrimp, and bread pudding doused in whiskey sauce are a few notables. Service just doesn't get better than at Mr. B's.

Signature dish: Bacon-wrapped shrimp and grits

THE MUNCH FACTORY, GENTILLY

Culinary Institute of America–trained chef Jordan Ruiz and his wife/partner, Alexis, proffer creatively imagined Creole cuisine and comfort food, including a dark-chicken-and-sausage-gumbo, shrimp and grits, and blackened Gulf fish. They have an outpost at the airport too.

Signature dish: Uncle Jo's pasta with shrimp, sausage, and fried chicken

PASCAL'S MANALE, UPTOWN

Now part of the Dickie Brennan Restaurant Group, this Uptown classic is known for a menu that combines Creole and Italian traditions, a mix of turtle soup and shrimp rémoulade with veal piccata and spaghetti and meatballs.

Signature dish: Barbecue shrimp

TABLEAU, FRENCH QUARTER

Elegant and dripping with architectural details, this Dickie Brennan restaurant spotlights regional ingredients and classic French Creole fare. Although there isn't a bad seat in the house, Tableau's seating along the wraparound balcony overlooking Jackson Square is stupendous.

Signature dish: Fried oyster pan roast

BANH MI BOYS

5001 Airline Drive, Suite B
Metairie, LA
bmbsandwiches.com

A SECOND GENERATION BLURS THE LINES ON TRADITION

The way twenty-five-year-old Peter Nguyen saw things back in 2015, the banh mi sandwiches he grew up with weren't living up to their potential. Despite having zero restaurant experience, the New Orleans native decided to buck tradition and stuff banh mis and po'boys with the likes of bulgogi, bang bang shrimp, and spicy Asian brisket.

His idea for Banh Mi Boys, a freewheeling po'boy and banh mi shop tucked next to a gas station in Metairie on Airline, wasn't to forsake the foods of his Vietnamese heritage.

The menu would include banh mi filled with pork meatballs, grilled lemongrass chicken and steak topped with a sunny-side up egg, and pork pâté. But he wanted to do more. Although his mom—who owned the gas station—thought it was a harebrained idea, he was a rent-paying tenant. After seven years, his mom's retirement was powered by Banh Mi Boys, and she became a believer.

Peter and others of his generation are interested in creating something new, drawing on traditional flavors but veering from traditional form. It's a formula that shows up in mom-and-pop corner stores and the Viet Cajun seafood boil joints around town.

Banh Mi Boys was a hit from day one and expanded with its first franchise, Uptown, on Magazine in 2021. Two more locations are in the works, in Killeen, Texas, and Columbia, South Carolina.

Like the original, all Banh Mi Boys serve sandwiches filled with five-spice pulled pork, Cajun garlic butter shrimp, or chicken katsu. Spicy Asian brisket is marinated with a dry rub and cooked low and slow for twelve hours, and then served with a tangy Asian barbecue sauce, cilantro, and the snap of julienned daikon and carrots for texture. The honey sriracha shrimp tosses fried local shrimp in the sweet heat of honey and sriracha.

In New Orleans, the banh mi sandwiches are served on Dong Phuong bread, while the po'boys come on Leidenheimer bread, two family-owned bakeries synonymous with the best sandwiches in town.

Along with starters like grilled pork or tofu spring rolls and crab Rangoon, the house-cut fries veer wildly from the norm. Other specialties are cheeseburger fries, roast beef debris fries, and oyster Rockefeller fries that can double as a po'boy. K-Town fries are another favorite, a belly-busting combo of marinated bulgogi steak topped with green onions, cilantro, and kimchi mayo. In the wings category, flavors hopscotch between traditional Buffalo and Korean barbecue to pho, made with a rub Peter created from spices including star anise, cinnamon, and cardamom.

The key to spreading the Banh Mi Boys gospel, Peter knew, was consistency. Thus, he created the banh mi bible. "I'm really just a home cook, measuring by eye," he said. "So, I broke every recipe down and measured everything to create formulas so the franchisees would be set up for success."

Cajun Garlic Butter Shrimp Banh Mi

CAJUN GARLIC BUTTER SHRIMP BANH MI

This recipe reflects chef Peter's culinary upbringing. A Vietnamese kid raised in New Orleans, he grew up eating popular food from both cultures. This sandwich is the prime example of what happens when the two worlds collide. The carrots taste best when marinated overnight, but if you don't have the time, even thirty minutes will do.

SERVES 2

2 TABLESPOONS SUGAR

1 TABLESPOON KOSHER SALT

2 CUPS RICE VINEGAR

2 CUPS JULIENNED CARROTS

½ CUP UNSALTED BUTTER, ROOM
TEMPERATURE

1 TEASPOON CAJUN/CREOLE
SEASONING

1 TEASPOON GARLIC POWDER

1 TEASPOON SMOKED PAPRIKA

1 TEASPOON CRAB BOIL SEASONING

2 TABLESPOONS FRESH
LEMON JUICE

2 TABLESPOONS MINCED GARLIC

2 TABLESPOONS MINCED SHALLOTS

4 LARGE EGGS

16 LARGE SHRIMP, PEELED
AND DEVEINED

2 CUPS ALL-PURPOSE FLOUR

½ CUP NEUTRAL OIL, CANOLA
OR VEGETABLE

2 (8-INCH) FRENCH PISTOLETTES
OR BAGUETTES

10 SLICES CUCUMBER

1 JALAPEÑO, SEEDED
AND SLICED THIN

10 SPRIGS CILANTRO

1. Whisk sugar and salt into vinegar until dissolved to make pickling liquid for carrots.

2. Pour pickling liquid over carrots in small bowl and refrigerate to marinate as long as you can, up to overnight.

3. Mix butter, Cajun/Creole seasoning, garlic powder, smoked paprika, crab boil seasoning, lemon juice, garlic, and shallots in medium-sized bowl until whipped in texture, 3–4 minutes.

4. Beat eggs in small bowl.

5. Dredge shrimp in flour, then in eggs, then coat one more time in flour.

6. Pour oil into frying pan and heat until medium hot and shimmering, about 2 minutes. Working in batches, fry shrimp until golden brown, 2–3 minutes per batch. Transfer to paper towels to drain. Pour off oil from pan.

7. Add Cajun garlic butter to same pan and cook on medium until butter melts and starts to bubble, 3–4 minutes.

8. Toss shrimp in pan until coated.

9. Toast pistolettes or baguettes according to your preference, and cut an opening along bread with a serrated knife three-quarters of the way through.

10. For each sandwich, add 8 shrimp, 5 slices cucumber, 3 slices jalapeño, a handful pickled carrots, and 5 sprigs cilantro.

BLACK ROUX CULINARY COLLECTIVE

2317 Burgundy Street
blackrouxcollective.com

EXPECT THE UNEXPECTED WITH SOUL

Chef Maya Masterson is a whirlwind of creativity. Whether she is marching in the Women of Wakanda Chewbacchus Mardi Gras parade, performing a song from *Cabaret* at a social justice charity event, or creating culinary experiences that see the forced African diaspora through a new lens, she's never predictable.

Maya's business, Black Roux Culinary Collective, includes immersive culinary tours; private catering, with a specialty in creative vegan cuisine; and regular seven-course curated dinner events in the lush, intimate courtyard at Hotel Peter and Paul. The boutique Marigny hotel and event venue transforms sacred spaces—including a Catholic church, rectory, and convent—into an oasis of hospitality.

The soul dinner series, like everything Maya does, is layered and multidimensional. The dinner, which she describes as "a seat at my ancestors' table," is choreographed with commentary from the chef between courses, an optional cocktail pairing, and, depending on the theme, live music, dance performances, or a DJ spinning a curated playlist.

"My goal is to create an immersive journey defining the food that came over to the Americas during the transatlantic slave trade," said Maya. "Soul dives headfirst into the cuisine developed by captive Africans and their descendants in the seventeenth and eighteenth centuries."

The dinner is designed to change the narrative regarding "slave food," she said. "Many ingredients and dishes have become popular, and some still have a stigma attached to them. This is my way of elevating these dishes and the ingenuity it took to create a cuisine out of necessity." Snout-to-tail consumption is not a new concept. Those fancy pig tails showing up on menus? Nothing trendy about that; same for chitterlings and neck bones.

At one of her recent dinners, the menu included watermelon tartare with groundnut mousse and cracklins. A whole-hog consommé was served with a marrowbone and cornbread tuiles. She also served a duck chitterling hand pie with dandelion green pesto and a dessert of forbidden rice calas with sweet potato agua fresca and buttermilk ice cream.

Maya launched her dinner series to uplift foods that deserve more respect, and to reframe the culinary conversation in a meaningful way. "Sorghum molasses was grown on plantations. I do a dish with fermented molasses and Louisiana popcorn rice, cooked in the style of sticky rice. These ingredients were considered slaves' food and then poor men's food. I imagine my ancestors looking down and smiling to see people choosing to eat this food."

A native of Detroit, Maya learned about cooking and growing food from her grandmother. After earning her culinary arts and management degree at Baltimore International College, she started exploring global cuisines in places like Seattle, Greece, Bangkok, and Peru. She worked in catering, hotels, and restaurants around the United States before settling in New Orleans in 2019.

Maya is known for her creative cooking style and riffs on traditional flavors. The cuisine she creates is intended to evoke emotion and be discussed. Her soul dinners are the embodiment of that aim. "I think this is important. That's why I'm doing it," she said.

COLLARD-STUFFED CORNISH HENS

This recipe is inspired by chef Maya's grandmother Lucy Curry and the giant collard greens that grew in her garden in Detroit. She was born and raised in Arkansas, so she was a country girl at heart, even in the city. Chef Maya remembers how huge the leaves of collard greens seemed when she was a little girl. She'd help her grandmother pick and clean the greens for Sunday supper, and in turn her grandmother would often use them to stuff Cornish hens, Maya's favorite kind of bird.

SERVES 4

2 CORNISH HENS

SALT AND PEPPER, TO TASTE

6 GARLIC CLOVES, MINCED

½ SWEET ONION, CHOPPED

½-INCH PIECE GINGER, PEELED

1 SERRANO PEPPER

1 TABLESPOON SEASONED RICE VINEGAR

1 TABLESPOON SOY SAUCE

1 TEASPOON LIQUID SMOKE

2 CUPS VEGETABLE BROTH

3 POUNDS COLLARD GREENS, RIBS REMOVED, ROUGH CHOPPED

1. Clean Cornish hens and pat dry. Sprinkle with salt and pepper inside and out. Place hens on plate, uncovered; refrigerate 2 hours.

2. Sauté garlic, onion, ginger, and serrano pepper until onion is translucent. Add liquid ingredients and bring to simmer.

3. Add collard greens, reduce heat, and simmer, covered, 20 minutes. Remove greens from liquid and cool. Use leftover liquid to baste hens as they roast.

4. Preheat oven to 375°F.

5. Stuff hens with cooled collard mixture. Tie legs together and place in roasting pan.

6. Bake 15 minutes, then turn heat down to 350°F and cook until done, about 1 hour, basting with reserved collards liquid every 15 minutes or so. Split hens, serving each person a half.

— THE BOWER

1320 Magazine Street
thebowernola.com

FARM-FUELED CREATIVE CUISINE IN THE LOWER GARDEN DISTRICT

Thankfully, The Bower had a second coming.

The verdant restaurant in the Lower Garden District opened for service on March 13, 2020. And like every other restaurant in the city, it closed its dining room on March 20, the date the stay-at-home order was issued because of the coronavirus.

After reopening to diners in 2021, the restaurant, from Latter Hospitality (Tujague's, Claret Wine & Cocktail Bar, Birdy's), managed to not just survive, but thrive.

Much of that growth can be credited to talented chef Marcus Woodham, a steady hand at the rudder of a perpetually lean kitchen team. Woodham's brilliant small plates, house-made pastas, and lovingly simple treatment of seafood and heritage meats invite regular discovery.

The word "bower" conjures a leafy country lane, a welcoming respite from city life, rich with greenery and ease. That's exactly the vibe at this modern farm-fueled eatery. Marcus, a Louisiana native, worked at Luke, Patois, and Galatoire's prior to joining Latter's ranks. He works closely with partner farm Sugar Roots to provide a menu featuring the best seasonal ingredients from the fields and garden. The Algiers farm grows some sixty different vegetables for The Bower's menu.

Everything at The Bower spotlights pristine ingredients and classic techniques, such as house-made pastas like rigatoni with ground shrimp and crab; tagliatelle with chicken saltimbocca, prosciutto, capers, and spinach; and paneed pork loin with mint, radish, avocado, and watermelon molasses.

The Bower is at once upscale and intimate, with acoustics and lighting that encourage conversation. Get a charcuterie board—a revolving array of meats and cheeses that might include 'nduja, a spreadable salami from Calabria, and the one-two punch of duck and date rillettes—ideal for dual nibbling. There's always a blue, perhaps Cabrales from Spain, along with an aged cheddar from Wisconsin and an earthy, soft French Brillat-Savarin.

The crispy cauliflower is revelatory, taken out for an Asian spin with Napa cabbage, chili oil, garlic, and cilantro. The basil spaghetti dishes up pesto squared, with basil inside and on top of the al dente pasta, bright with preserved lemon and a rich slick of burrata. There's always Gulf fish paired with mushrooms from Mushroom Maggie's Farm in a lobster and tomato broth shot through with citrus.

Cocktails are created with the same farm-fresh ingredients from Sugar Roots and are an exercise in both creativity and meticulous execution.

The Bower is a gem, a pleasure to discover. In a city where fried food and heavy sauces abound, this restaurant offers the solace of lighter, fresher, vegetable-forward cuisine with flavor to spare.

EGGPLANT PARMESAN

New Orleans has a long growing season, which seems to work particular magic on glossy Italian eggplants. Chef Marcus loves their hearty, meaty texture in late summer and long into fall. His eggplant parm is a departure, in that he fries and then bakes the eggplant with cheese, adding the spicy arrabbiata sauce spiked with fennel seed when plating. Braised Swiss chard adds an earthy tone that brings the classic to another level. Making the tomato sauce ahead is a time-saver.

SERVES 4-6

TOMATO SAUCE

3 TABLESPOONS EXTRA-VIRGIN OLIVE OIL

3 TABLESPOONS FENNEL SEED

1 LEEK, WASHED OF GRIT AND SLICED THIN, WHITE PART ONLY

¼ CUP CHOPPED GARLIC

½ CUP BALSAMIC VINEGAR

1 CUP RED WINE

4 CUPS SAN MARZANO TOMATOES

½ CUP TOMATO PASTE

3 TABLESPOONS DRIED OREGANO

2 TABLESPOONS DRIED THYME

2 TABLESPOONS GARLIC POWDER

2 TABLESPOONS ONION POWDER

3 TABLESPOONS SUGAR

SALT AND BLACK PEPPER, TO TASTE

1. Warm olive oil in sauté pan over medium heat. Toast fennel seed about a minute, then add leek and garlic.

2. Sweat vegetables until translucent, about 10 minutes.

3. Deglaze pan with balsamic vinegar and red wine. Reduce liquid until it's almost syrupy, then add San Marzano tomatoes and tomato paste.

4. Bring to boil, then reduce heat. Add remaining dry herbs, sugar, salt, and black pepper. Cook 15–30 minutes until sauce is thick. Adjust seasoning.

continued...

SWISS CHARD

5 BUNCHES, ABOUT 2 POUNDS, SWISS CHARD

2 TABLESPOONS EXTRA-VIRGIN OLIVE OIL

3 TABLESPOONS CHOPPED GARLIC

1 TEASPOON RED PEPPER FLAKES

½ CUP WHITE WINE

3 TABLESPOONS UNSALTED BUTTER

SALT AND PEPPER, TO TASTE

1. Remove big stems at bottom of chard. Cut chard in 2-inch increments and rinse under cold running water 5 minutes to remove any dirt.

2. In large sauté skillet or pot big enough to fit greens, heat olive oil over medium heat, then add garlic and red pepper flakes. Stir until fragrant, 1–2 minutes.

3. Deglaze pan with white wine and then add greens and butter. Cook until greens are tender and wine is reduced to almost dry, about 15 minutes. Season with salt and pepper.

BASIL VINAIGRETTE

½ POUND BASIL, STEMS REMOVED

½ CUP WHITE BALSAMIC VINEGAR

1 TABLESPOON HONEY

1½ CUPS CANOLA OIL

SALT AND PEPPER, TO TASTE

1. Bring large pot of salted water to boil. Make sure to have container with ice water close by.

2. Drop basil in boiling water 10 seconds, then immediately put basil in ice bath about 30 seconds. Remove and squeeze any water out.

3. Put basil, vinegar, and honey in blender, then slowly add oil to emulsify. Season with salt and pepper.

EGGPLANT

2 EGGPLANTS, PEELED

SALT AND PEPPER, TO TASTE

½ CUP ALL-PURPOSE FLOUR

4 EGGS, BEATEN

4 CUPS BREADCRUMBS

3 TABLESPOONS DRIED OREGANO

CANOLA OIL, FOR FRYING

OLIVE OIL, FOR BAKING DISH

1 POUND FRESH MOZZARELLA, CUT INTO ¼-INCH SLICES

1. Preheat oven to 400°F.

2. Cut eggplants longways about ½-inch thick. Season slices with salt and pepper.

3. Dust eggplant slices in flour, then dip into eggs, and finally in breadcrumbs seasoned with oregano.

4. In large, deep skillet, pour canola oil to a depth of ½ inch. Heat oil over medium heat until it registers 400°F.

5. Working in small batches, fry eggplant slices, turning once, until golden brown, about 3 minutes per batch. Using tongs, transfer to paper towel–lined baking sheet and season with salt to taste. Repeat with remaining eggplant slices.

6. Lightly brush 15 x 10 x 2–inch baking dish with olive oil. Layer eggplant slices with mozzarella. Bake until cheese is melted and bubbly.

To Serve

Place sautéed Swiss chard at bottom of plate; layer 2 pieces eggplant with tomato sauce. Drizzle basil vinaigrette around eggplant and be generous.

BYWATER BAKERY

3624 Dauphine Street
bywaterbakery.com

BAKING WITH LOVE AND COMMUNITY AT HEART

It was just so chef Chaya. As much of a community activist and rabble-rouser as she is an accomplished chef and bakery owner, Chaya Conrad had T-shirts printed up for Twelfth Night, January 6, the first day of Carnival season, and the exciting beginning of king cake season. "Confection not insurrection" marched across the front of the shirt in bold letters, atop a graphic purple, green, and gold king cake.

Leave it to Chaya—whose Bywater Bakery is a hub of neighborly spirit, giving back, and, of course, sweet and savory treats—to proclaim that love and pastry top mutiny any day.

Raised in Upstate New York, Conrad has worked in bakeries since she lied about her age to get a job at fourteen. A graduate of the Culinary Institute of America, she came to New Orleans to do her externship at Arnaud's. After working in a few other cities, she returned to Arnaud's as the restaurant's pastry chef.

The young chef's star was rising. After working at Dickie Brennan's Steakhouse, Chaya took a corporate fork in the road. She spent the next nine years overseeing Whole Foods' bakeries, where she created the brand's iconic Chantilly Cake. Next, she doubled down with the Louisiana-based Rouses grocery chain, managing bakery operations and creating the slightly tweaked Gentilly Cake, flavored with almonds.

But something was missing. Chaya, then newly wed to fashion designer Alton Osborne, wanted to get off the road and stay local. She was passionate about making a difference, one slice of cake at a time. The couple opened Bywater Bakery in 2017, just in time for king cake season.

The bakery immediately become a hive of neighborhood activity. An annual January 6 block party celebrating king cake season and live local music became a beloved tradition. Voter registration drives attracted political activists. Neighborhood kids got treats for good report cards. Business for special occasion and wedding cakes boomed.

In 2020, as a pandemic pivot, Bywater Bakery opened an outdoor service window, a lifeline of succor for an anxious community. Smiles and comfort were dispensed in equal portions with bake-at-home chicken potpies, croissants, and breakfast gumbo. The bakery's piano was moved onto a truck bed outside, along with tables, umbrellas, and outdoor speakers. Neighbors gathered for socially distanced live music to support out-of-work musicians. "We were all so starved for community and human contact," Chaya recalled.

As things returned to a new normal and the bakery gradually opened for inside business, the outside window remained a constant, along with a menu of sweet and savory morning pastries, a great Cuban sandwich, and cups of steaming ya-ka-mein, the best hangover antidote ever.

And always, through a lens of love and compassion, Chaya's and Alton's support for human rights stays front and center. The bakery proudly supports Black Lives Matter, pro-choice politics, Bakers Against Racism, Stand with Ukraine, and the New Orleans Musicians Clinic's Makin' Groceries program.

For anyone who thinks business should stay out of politics, Chaya begs to differ. "One of the beautiful truths about owning our own shop is that we can promote our values," said Chaya. "Even as we respect that your values may be different from ours."

CHICKEN POTPIE

At Bywater Bakery, two things have carried over from the early days of COVID. The community window remains; it was opened when indoor dining was shut down, allowing neighbors to safely order their favorite treats from this neighborhood hub. The other was chef Chaya's take-and-bake chicken potpies. What started out as a way to comfort and nourish the community has grown into a dinner staple in Bywater. It's a gift for sick neighbors, an act of love for the grieving, and an easy meal for a tired parent. It's the ultimate comfort food. Chaya's version is a little different, replacing peas with mushrooms and adding copious amounts of veggies and garlic. A splash of Marsala wine and a little lemon juice add a special twist. It's a delicious dish, but most importantly, it's food meant to be shared and served with love, which, along with "kindness matters," is Chaya's mantra.

YIELDS 2: 1 to keep, 1 to give away

CRUST

1 CUP COLD UNSALTED BUTTER	**1 TABLESPOON UNSALTED BUTTER, MELTED**
1½ CUPS ALL-PURPOSE FLOUR	**1 TABLESPOON CHOPPED ROSEMARY**
¼ CUP ICE WATER	

1. Rub cold butter into flour until pea sized. By hand is best.

2. Pour cold water into mixture and let sit 1 minute before mixing, so flour can swell without developing gluten.

3. Mix only until a ball of dough forms.

4. Separate into 2 balls and let rest in refrigerator a half hour before rolling out.

5. Roll out each ball into a 10-inch disk.

continued...

FILLING

¼ CUP OLIVE OIL	¼ TEASPOON BLACK PEPPER
2 MEDIUM ONIONS, DICED	1 SMALL SPRIG ROSEMARY
3 MEDIUM CARROTS, DICED	⅓ CUP MARSALA WINE
½ BUNCH CELERY, DICED	¼ CUP UNSALTED BUTTER
1 POUND MUSHROOMS, SLICED	¼ CUP ALL-PURPOSE FLOUR
2 TEASPOONS KOSHER SALT	3 CUPS CHICKEN STOCK
¼ CUP MINCED GARLIC	JUICE OF ½ LEMON
1 POUND CHICKEN BREAST, DICED	¼ CUP ROUGH-CHOPPED PARSLEY

1. In large skillet, heat olive oil over medium heat and add onions, carrots, celery, and mushrooms. Season vegetables with 1 teaspoon salt. Cook until tender, stirring occasionally. Add garlic.

2. In separate skillet, brown chicken seasoned with remaining 1 teaspoon salt, pepper, and rosemary. Deglaze pan with Marsala wine.

3. In medium pot, melt butter. Add flour to make roux. Add chicken stock and bring to boil.

4. Add vegetables and chicken to sauce. Squeeze in lemon juice and sprinkle in parsley.

5. Preheat oven to 375°F.

6. Divide filling between 2 prepared 9-inch pie pans.

7. Drape 1 crust evenly over each pie and crimp edges.

8. Brush with melted butter and sprinkle with rosemary.

9. Bake in preheated oven 1 hour.

CAFÉ RECONCILE

1631 Oretha Castle Haley Boulevard
cafereconcile.org

WHERE THE MENU'S MAIN COURSE IS HOPE

Having lunch at Café Reconcile is about so much more than eating some of the best shrimp and white beans in town.

Located in what was once a blighted building on Oretha Castle Haley in Central City, Café Reconcile pairs making a difference in the New Orleans community with a soulful dining experience. Chef Martha Wiggins took over the kitchen in 2021, bringing decades of experience to a job that goes beyond cooking soulful Southern cuisine.

Café Reconcile supports young adults, ages sixteen to twenty-four, helping them transform their lives through workforce development and training. This isn't only a culinary training program. Interns learn essential life and occupational skills, and are connected to support services such as mental health counseling, legal aid, health care navigation, and housing and childcare assistance.

They learn professional communication methods, résumé and cover letter writing, front-of-house hospitality techniques, back-of-house culinary techniques, and skills that can be applied in any industry. More than two thousand young people have been through the program, many of whom have gone on to work in the local restaurant and hospitality industry.

Martha grew up in Washington, DC, and started working at a neighborhood deli when she was fifteen. She went to culinary school and arrived in New Orleans in 2010, working her way to executive chef at Sylvain, where she was twice nominated for a James Beard Award. She worked with chef Alex Harrell as part of the opening team for The Elysian Bar at Hotel Peter and Paul.

In her current leadership role, Martha is aligned with Café Reconcile's commitment to equity and inclusion. She aims to effect change and create more equitable work environments that respect and reward the talents and contributions of all workers within a creative, diverse, and dynamic industry.

While always moving forward in this mission, chef Martha also wants to raise Café Reconcile's culinary profile. Her vision is to make it what she calls a modern soul food café. The restaurant's menu, served Tuesday through Friday for lunch, includes fried chicken, chili-glazed salmon, and po'boys stuffed with fried catfish, blackened shrimp, or crispy portobello mushrooms. Daily lunch specials—Friday's is smothered turkey necks with gravy—and sides like jalapeño cornbread, mac and cheese, and collard greens earn raves. The bananas Foster bread pudding is one winning dessert.

The inviting restaurant feels like an extension of mama's kitchen. The dining room is lined with photos of team members who have changed their lives through training in hospitality. Chef Martha's cuisine inspires an army of regulars. And her plan is to create a restaurant culture that raises the industry bar for how restaurants should look and operate in New Orleans.

Chef Martha fosters a culture of motivation, empowerment, and respect. As a Black woman leading a program that serves a mostly Black community, this position gives her the chance to truly effect change. As the executive chef of Café Reconcile, Martha can not only pursue her culinary passion, but also her desire to mentor and train young people.

SHRIMP AND WHITE BEANS

Shrimp and white beans has been a Café Reconcile staple for years, served every Thursday as the daily special. This is chef Martha's version, bringing the recipe back to the basics by using whole ingredients, slow cooking the beans, and cooking the shrimp to order so it stays fresh and tender.

SERVES 4-6

2 TABLESPOONS VEGETABLE OIL

1 ONION, DICED

1 GREEN BELL PEPPER, DICED

1 STALK CELERY, DICED

1 POUND DRY WHITE BEANS

2 QUARTS SHRIMP OR CHICKEN STOCK

1 QUART WATER

1 TABLESPOON CREOLE SEASONING

1 TABLESPOON WORCESTERSHIRE SAUCE

1 TABLESPOON HOT SAUCE

1 TEASPOON GARLIC POWDER

1 BUNDLE THYME SPRIGS

1 BAY LEAF

SALT AND PEPPER, TO TASTE

WHITE RICE, FOR SERVING

FRENCH BREAD, FOR SERVING

SHRIMP

2 POUNDS LOUISIANA SHRIMP, PEELED AND DEVEINED

CREOLE SEASONING, TO TASTE

2 TABLESPOONS UNSALTED BUTTER

2 GARLIC CLOVES, MINCED

¼ CUP WHITE WINE

1. Heat oil in large stockpot over medium-high heat. Sauté onion, bell pepper, and celery 5 minutes.

2. Add rest of ingredients (not the shrimp, rice, or bread) and bring to boil. Reduce heat to low and simmer uncovered, stirring occasionally, about 2 hours, adding water as needed.

3. When beans are tender, season shrimp with Creole seasoning and sauté in batches with butter, garlic, and white wine. Fold into white bean mixture.

4. Serve with white rice and French bread.

CAFÉ SBISA

1011 Decatur Street
cafesbisanola.com

CHEF SINGLETON BRINGS HIS LEADERSHIP FULL CIRCLE

Besides being an impressive Creole restaurant with stunning ambiance, Café Sbisa is one of the few fine dining restaurants in New Orleans with a Black chef as both co-owner and executive chef.

Chef Alfred Singleton is New Orleans born and bred. As co-owner and executive chef, he sees his role both as a steward for the circa-1899 grande dame and a means to uplift and mentor a crew that includes family and folks who might as well be. Café Sbisa offers a portal into what Creole cooking means to a chef who grew up in this city. Alfred started at the bottom, learning every aspect of the restaurant business firsthand. He wound up at the very top, adding his own interpretation to a cuisine that is as much a part of his identity as the Lower Ninth Ward, where he was raised.

A joyful celebration of Creole flavors rules Alfred's kitchen, from sherry-laced turtle soup and blue-crab cakes to the house special, trout Eugene, rich with a champagne cream sauce brimming with seafood.

The menu's emphasis on seafood is noteworthy. In a city famous for its seafood, Café Sbisa ups the ante on fresh. On any given day, depending on the season, Alfred might be contemplating a dozen soft-shell crabs or just-caught redfish, fresh from Hopedale, Louisiana. That's where his partner, co-owner Craig Napoli, runs his seafood dock and distribution business, ensuring guests pristine fish and shellfish on every plate.

Craig ran the restaurant from 1992 until Hurricane Katrina devastated New Orleans. He hired Alfred as a prep cook, but the cook worked his way up to head chef. With the city in recovery mode, Alfred spent a decade as executive chef at Dickie Brennan's Steakhouse. But his affection for Café Sbisa never waned. He approached his former boss with a proposal that the two work as partners and restore the restaurant to its former gastronomic glory.

Once an old ship chandlery, the restaurant's ambiance oozes romantic élan. The main dining room in the three-level restaurant is dominated by a handsome mahogany bar. Gallery seating overlooks the lively scene, with its bawdy mural painted by New Orleans artist George Dureau, a former regular. Thankfully, the striking three-panel painting somehow survived the mold that bloomed after the flood. Private dining rooms stretch across two more floors, with balconies overlooking Decatur Street and a courtyard for alfresco dining.

Chef Alfred has come full circle, now commanding the kitchen where he once stood in the corner chopping onions. He appreciates the work from every perspective, which makes Café Sbisa something special indeed.

BAYOU CRAB CAKES WITH CITRUS AIOLI

Chef Alfred loves making crab cakes to highlight the gorgeous blue crabs that are so plentiful in Gulf waters. The blue crab's scientific name is *Callinectes sapidus* which translates to "savory beautiful swimmer." Savory indeed, these Louisiana beauties are prized for their sweet, delicate flavor and tender meat and can be prepared in many ways, from steaming to grilling to sautéing in crab cakes like these, drizzled with an aioli with bright citrus notes.

SERVES 6

CRAB CAKES

1 POUND JUMBO LUMP CRABMEAT, PICKED OVER FOR SHELLS

¼ CUP CHOPPED RED ONION

¼ CUP CHOPPED PARSLEY

½ CUP FINE-DICED RED BELL PEPPER

½ CUP FINE-DICED GREEN BELL PEPPER

2 EGGS

¼ CUP CREOLE MUSTARD

JUICE OF 1 LEMON

¼ CUP PREPARED HORSERADISH

1 CUP MAYONNAISE

¼ CUP CREOLE SEASONING

1 CUP PANKO BREADCRUMBS

VEGETABLE OR CANOLA OIL, FOR FRYING

LEMON WEDGES, FOR GARNISH

1. Place crabmeat, onion, parsley, and peppers in large bowl.

2. In separate bowl, mix eggs, Creole mustard, lemon juice, horseradish, mayonnaise, and Creole seasoning.

3. Combine wet ingredients into crabmeat mixture, gently folding in breadcrumbs, keeping lumps of crabmeat intact.

continued...

4. Shape into crab cakes, each about ½ cup, and place on baking sheet. Cover and refrigerate at least 1 hour. This helps the crab cakes set.

5. When ready to serve, preheat large nonstick pan over medium heat and coat with oil. When oil is hot, place crab cakes in pan and cook until golden brown, 3–5 minutes per side. Be careful, as oil may splatter. Serve crab cakes warm with citrus aioli (recipe below) and lemon wedges for garnish.

CITRUS AIOLI

YIELDS 3 CUPS

4 EGG YOLKS

¼ CUP CREOLE MUSTARD

JUICE OF 3 LEMONS

JUICE OF 1 ORANGE

¼ CUP RED WINE VINEGAR

2 CUPS NEUTRAL VEGETABLE OIL

SALT AND PEPPER, TO TASTE

1. Combine all ingredients, except oil, salt, and pepper, in blender or food processor. Slowly add oil while processing to emulsify. Add salt and pepper to taste. If aioli seems thick, whisk in a little water. Store aioli in airtight container in refrigerator for up to 1 week.

CANE & TABLE

1113 Decatur Street
caneandtablenola.com

A RUM BAR WITH A CARIBBEAN CAJUN ACCENT

It's easy to walk right by Cane & Table, with its understated signage and the distractions that abound in this scruffy edge of the French Quarter. But that would be a sad mistake. This primo rum bar, with its bold Caribbean-meets-Louisiana cuisine, is one of the sexiest spots in town. Think date night supreme, with its ambient lighting, distressed plaster, and atmospheric back courtyard lit with twinkling fairy lights.

When it opened in 2013, Cane & Table was named one of the "Five Best New Cocktail Bars in America" by *Bon Appétit*. And no wonder, since the bar's pedigree is the real deal—it's the first official restaurant from the city's most influential cocktail entrepreneurs, Neal Bodenheimer and Kirk Estopinal, of the acclaimed and award-winning CureCo. bar and restaurant group.

With both a sophisticated bar and a game-changing restaurant, Cane & Table started out terrific. And with chef/partner Alfredo "Fredo" Nogueira steering the ship, it keeps getting better. Fredo also is a partner in the group's taqueria, Vals, and executive chef at Cure. At Cane & Table, he brings his Cuban roots into play with a menu that serves multiple masters.

Fredo, a native of New Orleans, has an innate appreciation of his hometown's cuisine. He learned to cook at his grandmother's side, stirring her pots as soon as he could reach them and experimenting under her loving oversight. He worked in kitchens as a teenager, starting as a dishwasher before graduating to the line. When Katrina displaced the chef, he went to Chicago, eventually heading the kitchen at a bar called Analogue, where he cooked what he knew: classic Louisiana food.

Fredo came home, eventually landing with CureCo. and directing the kitchen at Cure. The James Beard Award–winning bar is known for savory snacks with local flavor, perfect for pairing with its hyperseasonal craft cocktail menu. He was entrusted with the company's first foray into dining in the French Quarter as the leader of Cane & Table.

The restaurant's seasonally driven menu is inspired by Cuban influences, all the while drawing from the New Orleans lexicon. Dishes include ambitious Caribbean-inflected plates, like tostones with pikliz and habanero, curried fried pork skins, and traditional arroz con pollo infused with saffron. Fried Brussels sprouts deserve a tilde over the "e," thanks to a toss with cotija, hot sauce, aioli, and marcona almonds. Fish rundown, a dish popular in the Caymans, bathes local fried drum and crabmeat in a tropical coconut curry, all over Jazzmen Louisiana rice. As good as the rum cake is, choose flan for dessert. It was Fredo's abuela's recipe.

As for the drink menu, it's a marvel, from the authentic Hurricane to a spiced variation of the Manhattan, featuring bourbon and Jamaican rum. So often, first timers come for the drinks and then stay, thanks to chef Fredo's creative cuisine.

CRAWFISH CROQUETAS

This is a classic Cane & Table dish: Southern with a bit of Cuban influence. What's not to like about crawfish, béchamel, and fried goodness? If you poke around, you can probably find frozen crawfish tails in most places in the United States, but feel free to substitute cooked Gulf shrimp for the crawfish if you'd like. At the restaurant, chef Fredo serves this with garlic aioli for dipping.

SERVES 6-8

1 CUP UNSALTED BUTTER

1 MEDIUM ONION, DICED

1 CUP ALL-PURPOSE FLOUR

2 CUPS MILK

2 CUPS COOKED CRAWFISH TAIL MEAT, CHOPPED

½ BUNCH FLAT-LEAF PARSLEY, CHOPPED

JUICE OF ½ LEMON

KOSHER SALT, TO TASTE

CRACKED BLACK PEPPER, TO TASTE

CANOLA OIL, FOR FRYING

3 MEDIUM EGGS, LIGHTLY BEATEN

2 CUPS ITALIAN-STYLE BREADCRUMBS

1. In large skillet over medium-low heat, melt butter. Add onion and sauté until translucent, about 7 minutes. Add flour and cook, stirring constantly to ensure nothing sticks, until you have a sandy-colored roux, about 8 minutes.

2. Add milk in steady stream, whisking constantly to ensure it is well integrated. Reduce heat to low and cook, stirring occasionally, until liquid has become thick and tight.

3. Stir in crawfish meat, then remove from heat and stir in parsley and lemon juice. Season with salt and pepper to taste.

continued...

4. Coat baking sheet with thin film canola oil and spread crawfish béchamel mixture over it. Cover with plastic wrap to prevent a skin from forming, then refrigerate until chilled and firm, 1–2 hours.

5. When ready to serve, set up dredging station. Place eggs in one bowl and breadcrumbs in another. Season breadcrumbs with salt and pepper.

6. Roll chilled crawfish béchamel into 1-inch balls, then, working one at a time, roll each ball into breadcrumbs, dip into egg wash (allowing any excess to drip off), then roll once again in breadcrumbs to form croquetas.

7. In large, heavy-bottomed pan or Dutch oven, pour oil to a depth of 1½ inches and heat over medium-high heat to 365°F on a deep-fry or candy thermometer.

8. Working in batches to not crowd pan, fry croquetas, turning once, until deep golden brown, about 3 minutes. Transfer to paper towel–lined plate to drain, then repeat with remaining croquetas. Serve immediately.

THE CHLOE

4125 St. Charles Avenue
thechloenola.com

AN ELEGANT SETTING FOR MODERN AMERICAN CUISINE

Chef Todd Pulsinelli's roasted grouper is worth planning a weekend around.

Todd, the executive chef at The Chloe, a stunning little boutique hotel Uptown, creates the kind of cuisine that begs a double take. In this case, perfectly roasted local grouper is topped with pepper-charred oysters and bits of fennel atop a creamy sauce punctuated by ethereal smoked fish dumplings.

Then there's The Chloe Salad: royal red shrimp layered with Bibb lettuce and topped with crab fat and ravigote. Then again, the duck confit and apple salad with greens, pecans, jalapeño, and radish garnished with basil and mint beckons.

Clearly, the composed plates chef Todd is sending out of the kitchen at The Chloe are executed by a perfectionist. From the finest heirloom garnishes to the surprising layers of flavors, Todd's food sets a high bar.

The chef has spent more than twenty-five years honing his art. Born in Bitburg, Germany, and raised in Columbus, Ohio, where he went to culinary school, he moved to New Orleans in 2004. He worked at Domenica and American Sector, and also helmed the James Beard–nominated August for six years. In 2019, he joined the LeBLANC+SMITH team, where he now oversees The Chloe as executive chef, his fine dining chops firmly in place.

LeBLANC+SMITH is a class act, a hospitality company with integrity and committed leadership at the top. The company's mission statement says it all: "Focused on creating excellent 21st-century Southern hospitality experiences that enable all people to live joyful, balanced, and fulfilling lives and develop great leaders." The Chloe is LeBLANC+SMITH's first hotel, with restaurants and bars Sylvain, Anna's, Barrel Proof, and The Will & The Way rounding out its portfolio as of 2023.

The lushly revamped nineteenth-century property is set back from the street on St. Charles Avenue. Restored to a gorgeous luster after a yearlong redesign, the fourteen-room hotel opened in October 2020. The restaurant offers seating for 120 guests spread between the dining room and bar, verdant outside patio, and poolside.

The chef calls his cuisine eclectic—classics that he changes up just a bit. His agnolotti z'herbes with pot liquor and harissa sauce, for example: he braises collards in a spicy broth, stuffs the greens into pasta pockets, and tops the dish with ribbons of more greens. It's rich, elegant, and definitely not the traditional green gumbo. The menu mixes casual options like a royal red shrimp roll, a double-stack cheeseburger, and a chicken katsu sandwich with slow-cooked lamb shoulder and butter-crusted blackened drum. The Pork and Shrimp Étouffée Dumplings, served all day, are a version of a dish Todd served at August.

This chef-driven menu deserves close inspection. Forget dinner. Spend the weekend.

PORK AND SHRIMP ÉTOUFFÉE DUMPLINGS

Combining the comfort of shrimp étouffée with the Asian flavors of these pork and shrimp dumplings brings Louisiana goodness to an appetizer pretty enough for a special occasion. It's a little tricky getting the dumplings filled and sealed—better to under- than overfill—but the end result is worth it.

SERVES 6

PORK AND SHRIMP FILLING

1 POUND SHRIMP, PEELED AND DEVEINED, HEADS AND SHELLS RESERVED

1 POUND GROUND PORK

2 TABLESPOONS MINCED GARLIC

2 TABLESPOONS THINLY SLICED LEMONGRASS

2 TABLESPOONS MINCED GINGER

2 TABLESPOONS SAMBAL

1½ TEASPOONS CHOPPED CHIVES

45 CIRCULAR DUMPLING WRAPPERS

1 TABLESPOON NEUTRAL OIL, PLUS MORE AS NEEDED

¼ CUP CHOPPED CILANTRO, FOR GARNISH

1. Cover shrimp with cold water in large saucepan. Bring to boil and cook until just pink, 2–4 minutes. Drain. Dice once cooled.

2. In large bowl, add filling ingredients and mix to a paste.

3. Add 1 heaping teaspoon filling to center of each wrapper. Brush some water on wrapper around filling.

4. Fold wrapper into a semicircle, then pinch edges, ensuring that they are completely sealed.

continued...

5. In nonstick frying pan, heat oil over medium heat. When hot, add 10–15 dumplings, flat side down, and cook until browned on bottoms, 2–3 minutes. Add enough water to come just under a quarter of the way up the dumplings (about ½ cup), cover, and let water cook away until pan is dry and dumplings have softened completely, 3–4 minutes.

6. Remove lid, increase heat to medium-high, and let dumplings crisp up on bottoms for another 1–2 minutes.

ÉTOUFFÉE SAUCE

1 CUP NEUTRAL OIL

1 CUP ALL-PURPOSE FLOUR

RESERVED SHRIMP HEADS/SHELLS

½ CUP CHOPPED ONION

1 TABLESPOON MINCED GARLIC

1 TABLESPOON THINLY SLICED LEMONGRASS

1 TABLESPOON MINCED GINGER

8 CUPS WATER

1. In medium saucepan, heat oil over medium heat, whisking in flour to make a dark roux. Stir continuously until roux is color of dark chocolate, about 20 minutes.

2. Add shrimp heads and all aromatic vegetables to pot; stir another 3 minutes over medium heat.

3. Add water; bring to simmer. Adjust heat to medium-low and simmer 25 minutes.

4. Strain through fine-mesh sieve. Keep warm.

To Serve

Plate 5 or 6 dumplings per serving, top with about ½ cup étouffée sauce, and garnish with cilantro.

COMPÈRE LAPIN AT THE OLD NO. 77

535 Tchoupitoulas Street
comperelapin.com

CHEF NINA COMPTON EMBRACES HER ADOPTED CITY

Chef Nina Compton could have gone anywhere to further her meteoric career. But the St. Lucia native fell in love with the Big Easy in 2012, after she was the runner-up and fan favorite in Bravo's *Top Chef: New Orleans* (Season 11). She and her husband and partner,

Larry Miller, moved to New Orleans from Miami in 2015, when she opened her first local restaurant, Compère Lapin at the Old No. 77 Hotel & Chandlery in the Central Business District. The chef opened her second restaurant, Bywater American Bistro, in 2018, in the neighborhood that she calls home.

To say Compton has woven herself into the fibers of the New Orleans culinary scene is an understatement. The fact that she fell in love with New Orleans—with its culture, multiethnicity, and generational food traditions—is easy to see. Just talk to the lovely chef, who is universally admired and respected among her peers. She is a fierce advocate for women and BIPOC chefs and a vocal supporter and spokesperson for independent restaurants.

"I've never seen a city that so completely revolves around eating," she said. "For a chef like myself, that's huge. The appreciation for good food is massive." The pride in place continues to impress her. "Food has the ability to keep people resilient. Places like Miami and New York are transient. So many people are born and raised here. There's such a big heart and soul to this city. I wouldn't live anywhere else."

Her food is startlingly original, loosely anchored to her Caribbean heritage. Yet her culinary narrative is as improvisational as the jazz for which her adopted city is known. Compère Lapin, which earned her a James Beard Award for Best Chef: South in 2018, melds island flavors with chef Nina's love for French and Italian cuisine, while, of course, showcasing Louisiana's beautiful indigenous ingredients.

Compère Lapin's menu is as diverse and tempting as the city chef Nina calls home. One showstopping dish is her curried goat, a deeply layered stew studded with cashews and sweet potato gnocchi, bursting with flavors that crisscross the globe, from Trinidad to Durban. The seasonal menu may include a tuna ceviche with coconut, lime, and the crunch of jerk peanuts; fried chicken with jerk-spiced honey; dirty rice arancini; Jamaican brown stew with Gulf fish; or marinated shrimp resting in a cool, roasted jalapeño jus.

The restaurant's name is inspired by traditional Caribbean folktales Nina read as a child in St. Lucia, which featured a mischievous rabbit named Compère Lapin. Although her training is classically French, the chef conjures a playful menu that takes food that's familiar and deepens its allure. Now this is a food lover's dream come true.

ROASTED JERK CORN

Chef Nina loves sweet summer corn, and this dish reminds her of childhood summers on St. Lucia. The jerk butter, ranch breadcrumbs, and lime wedges make it a great seasonal dish at any dinner, gathering, or barbecue.

SERVES 8

JERK BUTTER

1 TABLESPOON CHOPPED ROASTED GARLIC (ABOUT 4 MEDIUM CLOVES)

2–3 TEASPOONS CAYENNE, DEPENDING ON DESIRED HEAT LEVEL

2 TEASPOONS ONION POWDER

2 TEASPOONS DRIED THYME

2 TEASPOONS SUGAR

1 TEASPOON CUMIN

2 TEASPOONS KOSHER SALT

1 TEASPOON PAPRIKA

1 TEASPOON GROUND ALLSPICE

½ TEASPOON BLACK PEPPER

½ TEASPOON RED PEPPER FLAKES

½ TEASPOON GROUND NUTMEG

¼ TEASPOON GROUND CINNAMON

1 CUP UNSALTED BUTTER, ROOM TEMPERATURE

8 EARS FRESH CORN, SHUCKED, EACH COB CUT IN HALF

RANCH BREADCRUMBS

1 CUP TOASTED PANKO BREADCRUMBS

¼ CUP RANCH POWDER SEASONING MIX

GARNISHES

1 CUP HOMEMADE OR STORE-BOUGHT MAYONNAISE

FINELY SLICED SCALLIONS, FOR SPRINKLING

CRISPY CHICKEN SKIN, FINELY CHOPPED, FOR SPRINKLING (OPTIONAL)

LIME WEDGES DIPPED IN CHILI POWDER, FOR SERVING

1. Heat oven to 375°F or heat grill to medium.

2. Bring large pot of water to boil.

3. In large bowl, combine garlic and all dry ingredients and then fold in butter.

4. Carefully add corn to boiling water and cook until just tender, 2–3 minutes. Drain well and, when cool enough to handle, pat dry. Brush each cob with jerk butter and wrap in foil. Place on large, rimmed baking sheet and roast until corn is heated through and butter has melted, about 8 minutes.

5. Meanwhile, make ranch breadcrumbs. In small bowl, combine toasted panko and ranch powder.

6. Remove corn from oven and remove foil. Brush again with jerk butter, then top with some mayonnaise and sprinkle with breadcrumbs. Sprinkle each cob with sliced scallions and chicken skin, if using. Serve with chili powder lime wedge.

BLACK CHEFS RISING

OWNING THEIR RIGHTFUL PLACE AT THE TABLE

Black chefs and hospitality workers have always powered the culinary experience in New Orleans. They just didn't get credit for it.

But that narrative is finally, slowly changing. Chefs and restaurant owners, including Nina Compton, Serigne Mbaye, Prince Lobo, Shermond Esteen, Manny January, Lisa Nelson, Charly Pierre, Alfred Singleton, Larry Morrow, and Edgar Chase IV, to name just a few, are expanding narratives about the origins of the city's cuisine. At the same time, there is a growing awareness of lifting up BIPOC team members and bringing them up through the ranks to deliver equity, diversity, and inclusion into hospitality spaces.

The fact that critical aspects of New Orleans culture track back to West African and Caribbean ancestors is expanding the conversation of what's on the plate. The human trafficking that accounted for one in every three residents being enslaved before the Civil War fundamentally influenced everything from music to iconic dishes like gumbo, jambalaya, and étouffée.

The year 2020 was a game changer. The pandemic dramatically pulled back the curtain on health inequities for Black and brown people. George Floyd's murder became a catalyst for change through the Black Lives Matter movement. Diversity, equity, and inclusion conversations weren't optional in the workplace anymore. That all led to an uptick of support for Black-owned businesses, including restaurants.

"When I first started this work seven years ago, no one was talking about it," said Lauren Darnell, executive director of the Made in New Orleans Foundation (MiNO), which as part of its mission focuses on scholarships, mentoring, and business coaching for those who are Black, indigenous, and people of color in the restaurant and hospitality business. MiNO also provides support to restaurant owners and hospitality companies that are seeking to eliminate bias in their organizations.

Making restaurants healthier places to work and more inclusive for Black and brown people is what Darnell calls "a gateway drug to inclusionary thinking. Creating a sense of belonging needs to extend to all marginalized people, regardless of factors including gender, sexual orientation, and ableism."

She sees the industry as being at last on the right path now. "We need to be telling the stories of true New Orleans hospitality and honoring the contributions of so many."

TWELVE NOTEWORTHY BLACK-OWNED RESTAURANTS

There are close to one hundred Black-owned restaurants in the city, from mom-and-pop corner stores dishing ya-ka-mein and po'boys to fine dining spots like chef Nina Compton's Bywater American Bistro. Here are a dozen spots not already mentioned in *City Eats*. There are many more to discover.

AFRODISIAC, GENTILLY

A mash-up between Shaka Garel's Jamaican roots and his wife, chef Caron "Kay" Garel's, foundation in southern Louisiana cooking. Try the Jamaican fried fish plate and the jerk chicken nachos.

BARROW'S CATFISH, CBD

Family owned since 1943, Barrow's third generation is now at the helm, keeping up with nonstop orders of signature fried catfish plates. All of the fried seafood is tasty—same for the barbecue shrimp.

HEARD DAT KITCHEN, CENTRAL CITY

Chef Jeffery Heard is a twenty-five-year hospitality veteran with deep fine dining experience. He now runs his own catering company and restaurant. Try the Superdome—blackened fish atop mashed potatoes and lobster cream sauce.

JAMAICAN JERK HOUSE, BYWATER/ST. CLAUDE

Richard Rose is Kingston born; his wife, Jackie Diaz, a first-generation Cuban American. Together they create top-notch Jamaican food, including jerk chicken and an oxtail ragù that always sells out.

LI'L DIZZY'S CAFE, TREME

The Baquet family's homestyle cooking has powered New Orleans family celebrations for decades. Now Wayne Jr. and his wife, Arkesha Baquet, are running Li'l Dizzy's Cafe in Treme. Get the fried chicken and gumbo.

NICE GUYS NOLA, GERT TOWN

Chef Darian "D Fresh" Williams worked at Emeril's for nearly a decade. He's passionate about his food, from a legendary gumbo to his stuffed turkey legs, crawfish crab cake, and chargrilled oysters. Bring a friend and get the way-loaded Earhart attack fries. Better yet, bring three friends.

NONNO'S CAJUN CUISINE & PASTRIES, MID-CITY

Chef Shermond Esteen Jr. ran kitchens in prison, as an inmate chef. After doing twenty years of a thirty-three-year sentence for possession of five ounces of marijuana, he came home to open Nonno's, first on Claiborne Avenue, then the Marigny, and now on Bayou ROad across from Addis. Get a plate of fried local jumbo shrimp, sautéed red snapper, or breakfast all day.

RED ROOSTER, UPTOWN

First opened in 1977 to serve snowballs, this tiny cottage in Central City expanded to dish hefty portions of overstuffed po'boys, ya-ka-mein, made-to-order burgers, and heaping seafood plates.

SAMMY'S ETHIOPIAN KITCHEN, MID-CITY

Opened in 2023 in the original Addis NOLA space, chef Sammy and his son Henok "Henny" Samuel offer authentic Ethiopian homestyle cuisine. Get the doro wot, a thick chicken stew, complex as a Mexican mole.

VAUCRESSON'S CREOLE CAFE & DELI, TREME

The Vaucresson family has been making sausages since 1899, with the third generation now running the business. Besides Creole hot sausage—a favorite at Jazz Fest—Vaucresson's serves crawfish sausage, alligator sausage, and jerk chicken sausage, all prepared as po'boys.

VYOONE'S, CBD

Vyoone Segue Lewis, a fourth-generation New Orleanian with Afro Creole and French roots, presides over Vyoone's (pronounced vee-ahn's), a hidden gem with its charming courtyard and an emphasis on local seafood with a distinct French accent. Try the crab cakes topped with crawfish cream sauce.

WILLIE MAE'S SCOTCH HOUSE, TREME

This Treme classic is one of the city's oldest Black-owned restaurants. Now in the hands of the fourth generation, Willie Mac's is famous for its crisp, batter-fried chicken, as well as dishes like mac and cheese, and red beans and rice.

DOOKY CHASE'S RESTAURANT
AND CHAPTER IV

LEAH CHASE STARTED GENERATIONS OF GOOD TROUBLE

Leah Chase left a formidable legacy when she passed at ninety-six in 2019. The Queen of Creole cuisine was short in stature, but she loomed large as a Black woman chef and restaurant owner, a civil rights advocate, and a supporter of women in the kitchen and out. She introduced one of the first Black-owned fine dining restaurants to the country, serving her signature Creole cuisine in an art-filled, elegant restaurant on the edge of Treme, America's oldest Black neighborhood.

Her many accolades included the 2016 James Beard Lifetime Achievement Award. Chase's portrait, painted by Gustave Blache III, hangs in the National Portrait Gallery of the Smithsonian. And she lives on, through her children, nieces and nephews, grandchildren, and great-grandchildren, many of whom are continuing to walk in her footsteps.

Her grandson Edgar "Dook" Chase IV oversees the restaurant's kitchen and, in 2023, opened Chapter IV in the Central Business District. Leah Chase's daughter Stella Chase Reese leads the family business, which includes a foundation concerned with social justice and education. Niece Cleo Robinson has been in Leah's kitchen since 1980, and Eve Haydel, also a member of the family's fourth generation, directs the bar at Dooky Chase's and now Chapter IV too. Great-granddaughter Zoe Chase is one of the newest working members of the culinary dynasty.

In the modern, art-filled Chapter IV, curated with the help of the Stella Jones Gallery, each painting or sculpture has meaning. "Each piece tells a generational story," said Edgar Chase. "It shows how we revere our elders." Each image shows a variation of matriarchs sharing knowledge with their young.

Chapter IV offers modern riffs on Creole cuisine, along with versions of Edgar's grandmother's Creole specialties. There are fish and grits, a fried chicken sandwich, crab and corn bisque, and a fried oyster BLT, a nod to the pork chop and oyster po'boy Leah Chase loved to eat while working at her busy kitchen.

The family celebrates the restaurant's eighty-third anniversary in 2024. Five years after her death, her grandson continues to be inspired by his grandmother. "Even if Leah Chase wasn't my grandmother, she'd be the most amazing woman I've ever known," Edgar said. "She'd always say, 'Keep working it to make it work,' and that's what I'm doing."

COPPER VINE

1001 Poydras Street
coppervine.com

A WINE-FORWARD OASIS OF MODERN CUISINE

The intimate wine experiences at Copper Vine are epic. A collaboration between two creative women, chef Amy Mehrtens and sommelier Emily Walker, the ongoing tastings and dinners are inspired by their curiosity and passion for food, wine, and genuine hospitality. Nothing stuffy to see here. Rather, the deep dives into wine are curated with fun in mind, at the same time providing insights into vineyards, varietal characteristics, and cellar practices that have given rise to some of the world's most satisfying wines.

First, the duo come up with a concept, perhaps showcasing a vintner with a compelling story to tell. After choosing wines, they unpack what's going on in the glass, features like color, flavor, structure, and aroma. From there, they'll reach for something less tangible about the wine, perhaps a memory evoked, a sense of terroir. The idea is to see an experience from the guest's perspective, to tell a story. And, always, mindfully pairing the wines with chef Amy's layered New American cuisine.

Once the concept is nailed down, Amy, a Culinary Institute of America graduate who is also a certified introductory sommelier, heads into the kitchen to play. The chef, whose résumé includes an early internship at the Biltmore Estate outside of Asheville, North Carolina, and working as a sous chef at Commander's Palace, strives always to balance flavors and seasonal ingredients at the imaginative intersection of food and wine.

Copper Vine is an ideal setting for this dynamic duo. The restaurant's historic space, which housed Maylie's Creole restaurant from 1876 into the 1980s, is airy and modern, and full of natural light, lush plantings, and local art. The handsome wooden bar on the first floor is a stunner, offering dozens of new and old-world wines on tap and by the glass. The multifloor restaurant, expanded in 2023, includes intimate dining rooms, private party rooms, and multiple kitchens, along with a leafy courtyard.

Growing up in a military family, chef Amy's love for cooking and curiosity about global cuisine began at a young age. She was born in Germany and spent time in Japan, California, Virginia, and Georgia. Amy came to New Orleans to check out the city's cuisine, and, like so many smitten visitors, she never left.

Copper Vine's menu is a portal into Amy's influences and inherent wanderlust. Her version of fried oysters might include nibs of pork belly, pickled okra, and blue cheese crumbles, with a Crystal hot sauce spicy glaze. Raw oysters come with a trio of sauces, a smoked bloody Mary, shallot mignonette, and preserved Meyer lemon hot sauce. Choices may range from seasonal roasted beet and Louisiana citrus salad to a grilled cheese plump with crawfish tails, or a smothered rabbit and mushroom fricassee swimming with pearl onions, root vegetables, and fresh thyme, with a buttermilk biscuit on the side. Always, the symbiosis between food and wine is ever present, making Copper Vine a destination-worthy restaurant in the heart of downtown.

EGGPLANT CAPONATA

This savory eggplant dish combines techniques from chef Amy's culinary journey since she moved to New Orleans in 2015. For this chef, every layer evokes a memory. As a cook, she sees herself as the sum of many experiences. A recipe on the Copper Vine menu might be hers, but it is conceived and executed thanks to techniques learned hand in hand with mentors, chefs, and friends. She feels lucky to have learned from so many great people, and dedicates this dish to them, with gratitude. At Copper Vine, she serves the caponata with burrata, drizzled with aged balsamic vinegar. You could do the same at home.

SERVES 4-6

EGGPLANT

3 LARGE ITALIAN EGGPLANTS
1½ TABLESPOONS KOSHER SALT

¾ CUP EXTRA-VIRGIN OLIVE OIL

1. Preheat oven to 375°F.

2. Rinse eggplants. Cut off stem end of each eggplant—no need to peel.

3. Dice eggplants into 1-inch cubes. Season with salt.

4. Place eggplants on rack over baking sheet and let sit at least 20 minutes.

5. Wring out excess liquid from eggplants by hand. This process helps the eggplants release their bitterness and makes for a better texture and flavor.

6. Toss eggplants with olive oil and roast on sheet pan 30 minutes, until tender all the way through and as soft as warm butter.

continued...

CAPONATA

¾ CUP EXTRA-VIRGIN OLIVE OIL

2 MEDIUM ONIONS, CHOPPED

4 RED BELL PEPPERS, DICED

4 STALKS CELERY, DICED

1½ TEASPOONS KOSHER SALT

1½ TEASPOONS BLACK PEPPER

½ CUP CAPERS

½ CUP QUEEN OR MANZANILLA OLIVES, ROUGH CHOPPED

½ CUP GOLDEN RAISINS

1½ TABLESPOONS STEEN'S CANE SYRUP

½ TEASPOON RED PEPPER FLAKES

⅓ CUP RED OR WHITE WINE VINEGAR

¾ CUP WHITE WINE

1 CUP BASIL, CHOPPED

½ CUP MINT, CHOPPED

½ CUP PARSLEY, CHOPPED

1. Heat olive oil in deep, wide frying pan on medium-high heat. Add onions, bell peppers, and celery. Season with salt and black pepper. Cook 5–7 minutes until translucent and tender, stirring often.

2. Add capers, olives, raisins, cane syrup, and red pepper flakes. Pour in vinegar and white wine.

3. Simmer 10 minutes on medium heat, allowing some liquid to reduce.

4. Stir in roasted eggplant and cook another 10 minutes. Adjust seasoning as needed.

5. Pull off the heat and cool at room temperature 1 hour.

6. Fold in basil, mint, and parsley.

COUVANT

317 Magazine Street
couvant.com

A NATIVE SON REIMAGINES FRENCH CUISINE

Couvant—a French restaurant in The Eliza Jane, a hotel in the Central Business District—opened in 2018, but it's had multiple personalities. It was a classic French brasserie when it first opened its doors in the striking brick stretch of redeveloped nineteenth-century historic buildings on Magazine. Once part of "newspaper row," the hotel is named for Eliza Jane Nicholson, one of the first women journalists to rise to the rank of publisher. At another point in its history, the building stored Peychaud's Bitters, the famous cocktail staple without which the Sazerac would never have been invented.

The French pedigree fits the gorgeous space, with its low lighting, tin ceiling, crushed velvet, and black-and-white tile floor. The opening menu sang with the likes of steak tartare, escargot, and foie gras. A gleaming marble oyster bar beckoned. Then March 2020 happened, and Couvant was shuttered for two years. This wasn't the kind of place that did takeout.

When the restaurant reopened in March 2022, a new chef was at the helm, New Orleans native Ryan Pearson. Adept in kitchens from France to New York, Ryan was sous chef at Daniel, the Michelin-starred French restaurant from chef Daniel Boulud in Manhattan. Couvant's second incarnation embraced French technique, but with modern, creative style. Ryan is rooted in New Orleans, so his allegiance to local dishes and the bounty from the Gulf burns brightly.

The chef's crawfish gnocchi are a wonder, a spot-on marriage of French and South Louisianan traditions. The potato gnocchi are crisped in brown butter and bathed in sauce Nantua, a creamy seafood sauce named for the town in southeast France where crawfish flourished. The chef combines crawfish stock and crawfish butter to build a sauce that is surprisingly light; it is served over the gnocchi with more crawfish, then topped with a garlicky chili crisp. There is still foie gras, but it's served with a Ponchatoula strawberry coulis. Gulf fish are front and center, but salmon is absent, because it's not sourced locally. The brioche-crusted veal entrée is based on a technique Ryan learned at Bâtard, the Michelin-starred restaurant where he worked in Tribeca in New York City. He rolls spinach-wrapped veal into brioche before cooking it in butter until crispy. The delectable result is served with cauliflower and king trumpet mushrooms and topped with sauce diable.

Couvant, from the French word for "smolder," offers a take on French cuisine steeped in refined simplicity. Both upscale and approachable, chef Ryan's reimagined French-Southern cuisine came at the right place, right on time.

ROASTED BEET SALAD WITH CREOLE CREAM CHEESE

Goat cheese and beets are French classics, but for this recipe, chef Ryan's menu of French-meets-Southern fare gives the traditional a reimagined twist. This salad adds Creole cream cheese to the usual chèvre. Similar to a combination of ricotta and sour cream, Creole cream cheese has a loose consistency, more like a burrata, adding a briny, creamy note to this delicious salad.

SERVES 2

ROASTED BEETS

5 MEDIUM RED BEETS

5 MEDIUM GOLDEN BEETS

1 CUP WATER

1 CUP WHITE WINE VINEGAR, PLUS MORE TO TASTE

2 TABLESPOONS NEUTRAL OIL, PLUS MORE TO TASTE

1½ TEASPOONS KOSHER SALT, PLUS MORE TO TASTE

¾ TEASPOON BLACK PEPPER, PLUS MORE TO TASTE

1. Preheat oven to 375°F.

2. Divide red and golden beets into separate roasting dishes and add water, vinegar, and oil into each dish equally. Season with salt and pepper.

3. Cover beets with foil and roast 1 hour.

4. Remove and cool to room temperature. Peel beets with paper towel; skins should come off easily.

5. Cut into bite-size pieces.

6. Season with additional vinegar, oil, salt, and pepper to taste.

continued...

CREOLE CREAM CHEESE MOUSSE

½ CUP CREOLE CREAM CHEESE, ROOM TEMPERATURE

½ CUP CHÈVRE GOAT CHEESE, ROOM TEMPERATURE

1 TABLESPOON MILK

SALT AND PEPPER, TO TASTE

1. Put all ingredients in food processor and season with salt and pepper to taste. Process on low until mousse has a spreadable consistency.

SALAD

10 TOASTED PECAN HALVES

4 STRAWBERRIES, HULLED AND QUARTERED

8 LEAVES ROMAINE LETTUCE, TORN INTO BITE-SIZE PIECES

SALT AND PEPPER, TO TASTE

2 TABLESPOONS WHITE WINE VINEGAR

1. Spread about 2 tablespoons Creole cream cheese mousse on plate in a circle.

2. Add half seasoned beets, pecans, and strawberries to each plate.

3. Toss romaine lettuce in bowl with salt, pepper, and white wine vinegar.

4. Add romaine to each plate and serve.

DAKAR NOLA

3814 Magazine Street
dakarnola.com

CHEF SERIGNE MBAYE'S STAR ASCENDS

When the 2023 James Beard Award finalists were announced in March of that year, Serigne Mbaye's name was one of six in the Emerging Chef category, a national honor for him and his new restaurant, Dakar NOLA. Although Serigne didn't win this time, his status as a winner, an accomplished chef whose moment is now, is indisputable.

Although it may seem that Serigne burst onto the national scene at the age of twenty-eight, the Senegalese chef is no overnight success. After traveling the world cooking at kitchens from Commander's Palace to the two- and three-star Michelin kitchens L'Atelier de Joël Robuchon in New York and Atelier Crenn in San Francisco, chef Serigne returned to put down roots in New Orleans in 2018.

When he arrived in NOLA, Serigne, who has family ties in Harlem and Dakar, felt an immediate sense of place. "It's the closest American city to Dakar," said the dynamic chef. Although he could have opened his restaurant anywhere, putting roots down into NOLA terra firma was a mindful move. "There is much in common between New Orleans and Senegal," he said. "The people here are kind, joyful; there is a strong sense of hospitality, which we have in Senegal too. There's crossover with food and music. Both places know how to celebrate around the table." He spent five years working pop-ups as Dakar NOLA, creating an evolving menu of Creole-meets-Senegalese dishes, shot through with French, Portuguese, and regional African influences.

His brick-and-mortar restaurant, which he opened in November 2022 with business partner Effie Richardson, is a thirty-seat jewel box Uptown on Magazine Street. The $150 chef's seasonal tasting menu brings Serigne's prodigious talent into laser focus. His cuisine stitches together influences of the African diaspora with a broader culinary narrative. The immersive experience connects the dots between history, continents, and cultures.

On one recent Saturday night, dinner included a mint froth–topped cup of traditional Senegalese tea, followed by the chef's take on what's known in Senegal as "last meal," a dish featuring black-eyed peas, which enslaved Africans were fed before their forced ocean crossing. A fonio salad is made with West African millet, finger limes, and an apple vinaigrette. Jollof, the Dakar-meets-NOLA cousin to jambalaya, is a course, as is yassa, a refined version of the spicy Senegalese dish made with habanero peppers, onions, and, in this case, red snapper. For dessert, jerejef is a free-form tart filled with a version of Gambian rice pudding, and topped with Senegalese green tea ice cream.

With Dakar NOLA, chef Serigne's vision is achieving its most complete heartfelt expression. His goal, beyond opening the restaurant, beyond achieving critical acclaim, is to raise up Senegalese cuisine, to give it a place at the table next to Italian or French cooking. And in his capable hands, it's working.

PECAN THIAKRY MILLET PIE

As a child in Dakar, chef Serigne's favorite dessert was a sweet spoonful of thiakry pudding. Thiakry is made with sweetened millet, a grain similar in texture to couscous. Available online as well as in specialty gourmet stores, the millet is traditionally mixed with milk, sweetened condensed milk, or yogurt, along with dried fruit such as raisins, plus coconut and nutmeg. This riff on that pudding combines one of the chef's favorite childhood dishes with a beloved Southern classic—pecan pie.

SERVES 8-10

1 READY-TO-BAKE PIECRUST

¼ CUP UNSALTED BUTTER

½ CUP SUGAR

½ CUP LIGHT CORN SYRUP

2 EGGS, SLIGHTLY BEATEN

1 TEASPOON VANILLA EXTRACT

¼ TEASPOON KOSHER SALT

¾ CUP CHOPPED PECANS, TOASTED

1 CUP COOKED THIAKRY MILLET

1. Preheat oven to 450°F.

2. Bake piecrust 5 minutes. Remove and set aside. Reduce oven temperature to 325°F.

3. In small pot, cook butter, sugar, and corn syrup over low heat, stirring constantly. Remove from heat.

4. Whisk in eggs, vanilla, and salt.

5. Stir chopped pecans and cooked thiakry into filling.

6. Pour filling into partially baked piecrust.

7. Bake 40 minutes, then cover crust edges with strips of foil so they won't burn. Bake 10-15 minutes longer or until set.

8. Cool pie 2 hours and serve at room temperature or chilled.

DEELIGHTFUL ROUX SCHOOL OF COOKING

1504 Oretha Castle Haley Boulevard
chefdeelavigne.com

CHEF DEE FOLLOWS A REVERED ELDER INTO THE SPOTLIGHT

At the Deelightful Roux School of Cooking in the fascinating Southern Food and Beverage Museum (soFAB), chef Dee Lavigne expects her students to roll up their sleeves and get to work.

Dee founded the city's only Black-owned cooking school taught by a New Orleans native in 2022, offering an informed deep dive into local lore, gastronomy, and culture as part of the experience. Her two-and-half-hour classes are hands-on, with students coached as they prepare an appetizer, entrée, and dessert.

A guided tour of the museum offers even more local history. Feasting and visiting are the savory grand finale, where students can choose to make dishes like gumbo, jambalaya, and shrimp and grits while enjoying lively chats about differences between Cajun and Creole cuisine and the real way to make a roux. Through it all, chef Dee's good humor, common sense, and personal stories make for an unforgettable, authentic experience.

Dee proudly follows in the footsteps of another Black woman, chef Lena Richard, who owned a cooking school in New Orleans more than eighty years ago. Dee first learned about Richard's accomplishments in 2017. At a time when Black people, especially Black women, faced the oppression and obstacles of the Jim Crow South, Richard was a chef, cookbook author, restaurateur, frozen-food entrepreneur, and cooking-school operator. She later became the first Black woman to host a cooking show on television, *Lena Richard's New Orleans Cook Book*, filmed in New Orleans, a decade before Julia Child became The French Chef.

Richard's life inspires Dee daily. Like so many successful creatives, Dee has ruled her career trajectory by saying yes first and then figuring it out on the back end. That's how she ended up with a degree from the Culinary Institute of America. How she worked in pastry at Whole Foods for fifteen years. And after the birth of her second son, it's what propelled her to launch her own baking business, Deelightful Desserts.

Along the way, Dee's earned plenty of accolades, including the Paul McIlhenny Culinary Entrepreneurism Scholarship through the Southern Food and Beverage Museum and the Big Top Carnival Baking Competition. She landed a regular Sunday-morning cooking spot on WWL, the local CBS affiliate station.

Between doing baking pop-ups, catering, four TV cooking segments a month, and running cooking and baking classes at SoFAB, Dee is busier than ever. In 2021, she also worked with the Smithsonian's "Cooking Up History" series to profile Lena Richard.

At the heart of it all, as it's always been, Dee wants to feed people.

"I want to make food and desserts that, when you eat them, it makes your soul smile," she said. "You can fake presentation, but you can't fake flavor."

Bread Pudding with Rum Sauce
See page 116

BREAD PUDDING WITH RUM SAUCE

Chef Dee was nine years old when her father asked his mother, chef Dee's late grandmother, Lorenza Raymond-Williams, to teach Dee the family bread pudding recipe. After just a few trial runs, Dee had it down. Custardy, moist, and rich, her grandmother's recipe strikes a perfect balance. Every time chef Dee makes this bread pudding, there are love, family, and memories of her grandmother in every bite.

SERVES 12-15

BREAD PUDDING

12 SLICES FRESH COUNTRY WHITE OR FRENCH BREAD

6 TABLESPOONS UNSALTED BUTTER, MELTED

1 CUP RAISINS

1 CUP SPICED RUM OR HOT WATER

3 LARGE EGG YOLKS

2 LARGE EGGS

¾ CUP PACKED BROWN SUGAR

1 CUP SUGAR PLUS 1 TEASPOON, FOR SPRINKLING

½ TEASPOON KOSHER SALT

1½ CUPS HEAVY CREAM

1½ CUPS WHOLE MILK

1 TABLESPOON VANILLA EXTRACT

1 TABLESPOON CINNAMON PLUS 1 TEASPOON, FOR SPRINKLING

⅛ TEASPOON NUTMEG

½ CUP CRUSHED PINEAPPLE

1. Preheat oven to 200°F.

2. Slice bread into 1-inch cubes and put half into large bowl. Place remaining half on baking sheet and bake 20 minutes, then let cool. You can also leave the bread out overnight to dry out if you have the time.

3. Increase oven temperature to 350ºF. Use melted butter to coat a 13 x 9 x 2-inch baking dish.

4. Soak raisins in spiced rum or hot water 10 minutes, drain, and set aside. (Save rum for rum sauce.)

5. In medium bowl, mix egg yolks and eggs well. Add both sugars and salt, mixing until completely dissolved.

6. To egg mixture, add heavy cream, milk, vanilla, cinnamon, and nutmeg.

7. Pour liquid mixture on top of fresh bread cubes and mix until all bread is broken down and completely mixed in. Sprinkle in soaked raisins and pineapple, then toss.

8. Add dried bread to wet bread mixture, toss, and let soak 30 minutes.

9. Pour bread mixture into prepared baking dish. Spread mixture evenly in pan.

10. Sprinkle top with 1 teaspoon each sugar and cinnamon.

11. Bake at 350ºF 65–75 minutes or until top of bread pudding springs back after lightly touching it with fork.

12. Allow to cool 10 minutes, cut into squares, and serve topped with rum sauce.

RUM SAUCE

¼ CUP UNSALTED BUTTER

½ CUP HEAVY CREAM, PLUS MORE AS NEEDED

⅓ CUP PACKED BROWN SUGAR

¼ CUP SUGAR

½ TEASPOON KOSHER SALT

¼ CUP SPICED RUM

1. Combine all ingredients in small saucepan over medium heat and simmer until sauce thickens, 10–12 minutes. Remove from heat.

2. Sauce will continue to thicken as it cools. If it gets too thick, add 1 tablespoon heavy cream or milk to thin it.

3. Pour immediately over bread pudding and serve.

DEL PORTO RISTORANTE

501 E. Boston Street
Covington, LA
delportoristorante.com

GAME-CHANGING ITALIAN FARE IN DOWNTOWN COVINGTON

It's been more than two decades since wife-husband team Torre and David Solazzo opened Del Porto Ristorante in Covington, helping to blaze a trail that's turned this sweet, walkable downtown into a genuine dining destination.

Located about an hour from New Orleans across Lake Pontchartrain, Del Porto reflects the couple's shared love for rustic Italian cuisine. The pair met while working at the Tra Vigne restaurant in Napa. Torre, a New Orleans native, is a graduate of the California Culinary Academy in San Francisco; David graduated from the Culinary Institute of America. They married in New Orleans in 2000 and worked at restaurants on the north shore of the lake, an experience that solidified where they wanted to raise a family and open a restaurant.

What started as a ten-table Italian café grew up and out, and the establishment moved into a larger downtown location on Boston Street, which then took over a neighboring storefront. The sleek dining room is perpetually crowded, and is a welcoming space that exudes warmth. In New Orleans, Italian food usually means Creole Italian, heavy with red sauce and cheese, with riffs on dishes brought to New Orleans by the large Sicilian population that settled in the city in the late nineteenth century.

But that's not the kind of food Del Porto serves. With a menu that is attentively seasonal, and an array of dishes that salute Italian regional cooking traditions, Del Porto is easily one of the best Italian restaurants on either side of the twenty-four-mile causeway. This is the place for handmade pappardelle, rabbit ragù, and duck confit ravioli, dishes that weren't in the mainstream NOLA restaurant lexicon in the early 2000s. The aromas of fresh herbs, citrus, garlic, and olive oil radiate in the space.

On any given night, there might be warm, house-made mozzarella with white Sicilian anchovy, basil, and confit tomato. Mussels get a Calabrese treatment, simmered with garlic, crispy sausage from the region, chili oil, and white wine. A grilled heritage pork chop is served with southern field beans and wilted greens. Short ribs are slow braised in red wine. For dessert, guests may enjoy a slice of rum-soaked Italian wedding cake or a creamy tiramisu.

In 2021, the couple channeled a different kind of energy and opened The Greyhound, a globe-trotting gastropub where the Greyhound bus station used to operate downtown. "We wanted a place that served the kind of food we crave when we're not working," said Torre. A hit from day one, the airy pub features an international beer selection, a wood-burning pizza oven, and an all-day menu with flavors that are idiosyncratic but familiar at the same time. The Greyhound features Reuben on rye with house-made pastrami and North African spiced lamb meatballs with polenta croutons. Gulf fish and chips might be a thick slab of fried drum served with crispy fries, a harissa aioli, and vinegar for dipping on the side.

The pair, surviving and thriving despite the challenges of recent years, see The Greyhound as a concept that deserves replication, maybe even on the other side of the lake. As for Del Porto, it will always be their first baby.

LEMON-MASCARPONE RISOTTO WITH GULF SHRIMP

To chef Torre's way of thinking, this elegant, comforting dish epitomizes the philosophy of Del Porto in one bite. Local ingredients shine through, with Italian techniques used to showcase food in its simplest form. This dish, when executed properly, marries the very best of Italian cooking with world-famous seafood from the Louisiana Gulf. Arborio rice is an important ingredient here. Because of its high starch content, it produces a creamier, more luscious rice with just the right chew.

SERVES 6

LEMON-MASCARPONE RISOTTO

1 TABLESPOON OLIVE OIL

½ MEDIUM ONION, FINELY DICED

1½ CUPS ARBORIO RICE

1 BAY LEAF

1 TABLESPOON GRATED LEMON ZEST

¾ CUP WHITE WINE

½ CUP FRESH LEMON JUICE

COARSE SALT AND WHITE PEPPER, TO TASTE

1 QUART HOT CHICKEN STOCK, PLUS MORE AS NEEDED

3 TABLESPOONS MASCARPONE

1. Heat oil over medium heat in heavy-bottomed stockpot. Add onion and sauté until translucent.

2. Add arborio rice and toast 5 minutes.

3. Add bay leaf, lemon zest, white wine, and lemon juice. Season with salt and white pepper, and reduce heat to simmer. Stir often, scraping bottom of pan until liquid is absorbed.

4. Add 1 cup hot stock and stir constantly with wooden spoon. The constant stirring is what makes the rice creamy.

5. When liquid is evaporated, add another cup hot stock and continue to stir until evaporated. Repeat this step until the whole quart of stock has been used. If rice is still too hard after entire quart of stock has been used, use extra stock. Rice takes approximately 20 minutes of constant stirring; it is ready when tender but slightly al dente.

6. Stir in mascarpone until combined.

continued...

SAUTÉED GULF SHRIMP

3 CUPS SHRIMP STOCK
(SEE RECIPE, RIGHT)

2 TABLESPOONS NEUTRAL OIL
(LIKE VEGETABLE OR GRAPE SEED),
PLUS MORE AS NEEDED

3 POUNDS LARGE GULF SHRIMP,
PEELED AND DEVEINED; KEEP TAILS
ON, RESERVE SHELLS

2 TABLESPOONS WHITE WINE

2 GARLIC CLOVES, SLICED

1 TABLESPOON CHOPPED BASIL

1 TABLESPOON CHOPPED CHIVES

2 TABLESPOONS UNSALTED BUTTER

1. Prepare Shrimp Stock.

2. Heat oil in large sauté pan over medium heat. Add shrimp and sear on both sides. Remove from pan. Shrimp should not be cooked all the way.

3. Deglaze pan with white wine. Add Shrimp Stock, garlic, and herbs and bring to simmer. Reduce by half.

4. Add butter to simmering sauce to emulsify. Add shrimp to sauce. Toss in sauce to warm through.

5. Split risotto evenly among 6 plates. Place 5–6 cooked shrimp on each plate on top of risotto. Spoon sauce over shrimp and serve.

SHRIMP STOCK

3 POUNDS SHRIMP SHELLS

1 SMALL ONION, QUARTERED

2 STALKS CELERY, CHOPPED INTO
1-INCH PIECES

6 PARSLEY STEMS

1 BAY LEAF

2 LEMONS, SLICED

1. Preheat oven to 400°F.

2. Toast shrimp shells on sheet pan in oven 10 minutes or until red and dry.

3. In stockpot, combine all ingredients, cover with water, bring to boil, then lower heat. Simmer approximately 45 minutes. Strain and set aside.

8 FRESH FOOD ASSASSIN RESTAURANT & LOUNGE

1900 N. Claiborne Avenue
8freshfoodassassin.com

A CHEF WHO KILLS IT, EVERY TIME

A sign in chef Manny January's restaurant, 8 Fresh Food Assassin, says "Everyday I'm hustlin."

This mantra has propelled this soft-spoken, modest chef through the ranks of one of New Orleans's storied Creole restaurants, to working for himself by cooking on the street at parades, to finally opening his own restaurant in 2022.

This compact eatery is in the Seventh Ward on North Claiborne Avenue, a stand-alone storefront by the shops and clubs on the busy stretch near Elysian Fields.

Manny explains the restaurant's name this way: "I'm from the Eighth Ward, my first menu had eight dishes, I cook fresh, and I assassinate it."

He does indeed. Manny got into trouble as a teenager and served two years in jail for theft. On the fifth day after his release, he applied for a job as a dishwasher at Galatoire's, a fixture on Bourbon Street since 1905. Despite having no formal culinary education, Manny was promoted quickly, moving up the ranks in the busy kitchen, working stations including the fryer, grill, and broiler with skill and efficiency. He was one of the small crew that got Galatoire's open after Katrina, often juggling multiple jobs at once. Altogether, he worked there for seventeen years. His last role was sous chef, often charged with the responsibility of representing the restaurant on the road and at festivals.

Manny's combination of fine dining chops and street smarts propelled this natural entrepreneur forward. He started working for himself under the name Da Street Kitchen as an outdoor food vendor, selling fish and shrimp plates from the back of a truck during second lines. Then he started setting up outside nightclubs, feeding hungry patrons, with folks lined up and waiting. He debuted his eight-item menu at The Association, a club on North Claiborne. He couldn't keep up with the demand. Manny knew he needed a brick-and-mortar restaurant to serve his community.

That restaurant turned out to be a newly vacated space directly across the street from The Association. Manny, whose Instagram following is at 25K and climbing, opened for business in May 2022. From the jump, his menu stood out from the crowd. Grilled lamb chops, marinated for flavor and cooked with just a hint of char, became a crowd favorite, something not seen at most restaurants in the neighborhood. He still has fried seafood platters, along with oversized T-bone steaks, tender fried ribs, and grilled salmon with a sweet hot honey barbecue sauce. Seafood-stuffed potatoes, homestyle mac and cheese, and greens are a few more options, and there's always a special. Like the sign says, chef Manny is always hustlin', the surefire recipe for his success.

MARINATED GRILLED LAMB CHOPS

Although his menu includes lots of down-home New Orleans dishes, chef Manny's regulars come back, again and again, for his chargrilled lamb chops, usually with a creamy seafood potato on the side. When he opened his casual neighborhood restaurant in 2022, he wanted to introduce the community to this favorite special from his days at Galatoire's, a dish they may not have tried before. Selling one order a day turned into selling twenty cases a week. Now those tender, marinated chops are his calling card. He cuts and cleans the chops first, seasons them—assassin style—and marinates them in Italian dressing for twenty-four to forty-eight hours. These savory chops are grilled to order, although, if asked, chef Manny recommends them medium rare.

SERVES 6

2 CUPS ITALIAN DRESSING	1½ TEASPOONS KOSHER SALT
1 CUP DALE'S LIQUID SEASONING	½ TEASPOON BLACK PEPPER
2 TEASPOONS MCCORMICK STEAK SEASONING	1 TEASPOON DRIED PARSLEY FLAKES
½ TEASPOON GARLIC POWDER	12 AMERICAN LAMB LOIN CHOPS, 1 INCH THICK, OR LAMB RIB CHOPS
½ TEASPOON ONION POWDER	

1. Place Italian dressing and Dale's Seasoning in bowl, stirring well to combine.

2. In separate small bowl, combine remaining seasonings to make spice mix.

3. Place chops in nonreactive dish and season both sides with spice mix. Pour liquid marinade over meat, cover, and refrigerate 24 to 48 hours.

4. Remove lamb chops from refrigerator 30 minutes before cooking them.

continued...

5. When ready to cook, heat gas grill to 500°F and grill chops 5–7 minutes per side, until internal temperature reaches 135°F–145°F for medium rare to medium. Or preheat broiler to high and broil chops about 8 inches from heat source, 5 minutes per side.

6. Remove chops from broiler or grill, place on platter, and let rest, loosely tented under foil. During this time, juices redistribute throughout meat. After resting, plate and serve immediately.

THE ELYSIAN BAR

2317 Burgundy Street
theelysianbar.com

DINING AS A RELIGIOUS EXPERIENCE

For the food obsessed, restaurant dining is devotional, an ongoing pilgrimage to favorite cuisines, chefs, and immersive experiences.

At The Elysian Bar in the raptly renovated seventy-one-room Hotel Peter and Paul, the sacred setting of the hotel's rectory combines with chef Kyle Focken's fresh-forward European cuisine to take guests on a one-of-a-kind dining experience.

The Elysian Bar is from the same folks who run the innovative Bacchanal in Bywater, an outdoor yard party where glee, wine, charcuterie, and global eats are served in equal measure. The cocktail and wine list impresses at The Elysian Bar, with its apostolic-chic vibe and design of vibrant colors, textures, and patterns. Diners have a choice of fab spaces in which to sup—the rectory, bricked church courtyard, two comfy parlors, or the light-filled atrium. The place drips with architectural and design details, from floor-to-ceiling pooled draperies to vaulted ceilings, Italian marble, and chandeliers. The setting is spectacular, with the renovated church the pièce de résistance, a grand sacred space perfect for social events and weddings.

In year one, with chef Alex Harrell in the kitchen, The Elysian Bar scored a Best New Restaurant nomination by the James Beard Foundation in 2019, along with a place on *Bon Appétit*'s Hot 10 New Restaurants list. The bar program won them a place on *Esquire*'s Best Bars in America list in 2021. Alex laid a super foundation before moving on to opening his own restaurant, Angeline. He's now leading the culinary offerings at the Virgin Hotels New Orleans.

Kyle brings a fresh eye to The Elysian Bar's forward-looking menu. The chef started in the restaurant industry washing dishes as a teenager, moving into the kitchen at eighteen. He learned on the job, working alongside excellent chefs at places like DTB, The Franklin, and LUVI.

The chef's focus is on a health-conscious menu, creating dishes evoking French cuisine with Spanish undertones. Local, seasonal produce is always in the mix, with the idea to refresh and satisfy his guests without weighing them down with rich, heavy sauces. Noteworthy dishes include crab and ricotta gnocchi with Calabrian chile peppers and bottarga breadcrumbs; and oven-roasted bone marrow with cashew, pickled Chioggia beet, and mint.

Before or after dinner, the splendid Henry Howard–designed buildings that make up Hotel Peter and Paul deserve closer inspection. Spanning multiple structures, including the former church school building as well as a rectory and convent, the space was transformed by a two-year renovation into a chic, tucked-away stay. Each building has its narrative, ensuring that no two guest rooms are exactly alike. The place is abundantly romantic, from the canopied beds and marble bathrooms to the curated antique and bespoke furnishings. Outside, a lush courtyard invites, with ivy-covered walls and a church bell towering in the background.

GRILLED LOUISIANA BUTTERNUT SQUASH

This vegetarian dish is simple but packed with big flavor. The Sunflower But-ter and buttermilk reduction add a creamy, silky finish that complements the squash seamlessly. The simplicity and refinement of this dish is a perfect fit for The Elysian Bar, which is a study in understated elegance in the Hotel Peter and Paul. Any leftover buttermilk reduction makes a perfect base for a creamy salad dressing.

SERVES 4

BUTTERMILK REDUCTION

1 QUART BUTTERMILK	JUICE OF 2 LEMONS
1 TEASPOON KOSHER SALT	

1. Add buttermilk to medium saucepan and simmer over low heat until reduced by half, approximately 1 hour. Buttermilk will separate, but don't worry, that is part of the process.

2. Once reduced, add buttermilk, salt, and lemon juice to blender and blend on high until mixture is spun back together, about 2 minutes.

BUTTERNUT SQUASH

2 BUTTERNUT SQUASH	1 TEASPOON PAPRIKA
3 TABLESPOONS OLIVE OIL	SUNFLOWER BUTTER (PAGE 134)
1 TEASPOON KOSHER SALT	SHISO OR CILANTRO, FOR GARNISH
1 TEASPOON BLACK PEPPER	

1. Preheat oven to 350°F.

2. Cut off top and bottom of squash and remove skin with vegetable peeler. Cut squash vertically, directly down middle, and use a spoon to scoop out seeds.

3. Lightly season all over with 2 tablespoons olive oil and salt, pepper, and paprika.

4. Place squash in baking dish, cover with foil, and roast 45 minutes or until fork-tender. While squash is baking, prepare Sunflower Butter. Remove squash from oven and let cool.

5. Remove foil and cut squash into 1-inch-thick slices.

6. Lightly drizzle with 1 tablespoon olive oil and, using heated grill or grill pan, grill squash on both sides.

continued...

SUNFLOWER BUTTER

2 CUPS RAW SUNFLOWER SEEDS

½ CUP PLUS 2 TABLESPOONS OLIVE OIL

½ CUP PICKLED JALAPEÑOS

JUICE AND GRATED ZEST OF 1 LIME

½ TEASPOON PAPRIKA

½ CUP SUGAR

¼ CUP HONEY

1 CUP WATER

KOSHER SALT, TO TASTE

1. Toss sunflower seeds in 2 tablespoons olive oil and toast in dry pan over medium heat until golden brown.

2. Deseed and remove any stems from pickled jalapeños.

3. Reserve a few whole sunflower seeds for plating. Place remaining toasted sunflower seeds and jalapeños in blender or food processor.

4. Mix lime juice, lime zest, and paprika with sugar, then add to sunflower seed mixture.

5. Add honey, then slowly add remaining olive oil and water, blending until smooth.

6. Season with salt.

To Serve

1. For each plate, place 1 tablespoon sunflower butter.

2. Add 1 tablespoon buttermilk reduction directly on top of Sunflower Butter.

3. Place 1 piece grilled squash on top of both sauces.

4. Garnish with shiso or cilantro and remaining toasted sunflower seeds.

WOW HOTEL DINING

Gone are the days when cavernous hotel restaurants were mere shadows of the real thing. Light-years away from a big-box amenity, many hotel restaurants in New Orleans deliver a strong sense of place meant to attract locals, not just visitors. Whether for a sexy date night or a milestone party, these destination restaurants impress. No hotel key required.

BAR MARILOU, CBD

Bar Marilou is part of the French-owned Maison de la Luz, a boutique hotel from Atelier Ace in the CBD. Order French-inspired snacks (olives, shishito peppers, frog legs), along with a Wagyu burger, roast duck with seared greens, and scallops. Deep-red walls, dramatic art, and amazing cocktails resonate with a speakeasy vibe.

CHEMIN À LA MER, FRENCH QUARTER

Step out onto Chemin à la Mer's fifth-floor patio overlooking the Mississippi and be gobsmacked. The only way to get closer to the river is to dive in—the views are that spectacular. It's what convinced chef Donald Link to partner with the Four Seasons Hotel New Orleans for this French Creole showplace, with its name that means "pathway to the seas." Taking inspiration from the Clover Grill steak house in Paris, diners can tuck into a rib eye spinalis or Kobe strip steak, along with Ōra King salmon with lentils, Gulf Coast ceviche, and duck confit with spicy greens.

COMMONS CLUB, CBD

Glamour-pusses flock to the slyly retro Commons Club at the Virgin Hotels New Orleans, a fab setting to showcase local chef Alex Harrell's enticing menu of Southern, seasonal, and Mediterranean-kissed small and large plates. Ask for a seat in the sexy Shag Room and bar area, where a riot of colors and textures surrounds you, and naked-as-a-jaybird art spreads across the walls and up the stairs to the second floor. Try the Gulf fish with Two Brooks Farm rice grits, preserved tomatoes beurre blanc, and lima beans.

THE GRILL ROOM AT THE WINDSOR COURT, CBD

Classy and sophisticated, The Grill Room promises a memorable dining experience worthy of a marriage proposal. Expect a scrumptious array of contemporary Louisiana dishes and extraordinary presentations. Executive chef Vlad Kogan and chef de cuisine Alex Kuzin preside over an au courant menu with dishes like seared scallops with compressed apple and crawfish cream and short rib pappardelle with a spiced port demi-glace. The $28 lunch special, a main and three sides, is perfection.

JOSEPHINE ESTELLE, CBD

James Beard Award–nominated chefs Andy Ticer and Michael Hudman power this Southern-inspired kitchen in Ace Hotel New Orleans with a menu that unlocks the full potential of its ingredients. Favorites include roasted oysters with Calabrian chili butter and signature house-made pastas, including the outstanding tajarin: silky thin strands tangled with crabmeat, butter, and asparagus. There's always a Gulf fish or a strip steak for the ravenous.

KING BRASSERIE & BAR, CBD

As if the befeathered Peacock Room at the Kimpton Hotel Fontenot wasn't sexy enough, the 2023 opening of King Brasserie upped the hotel's game, bigtime. For starters, it's so much fun guessing who's who in the king-inspired portraits and silhouette art that line the walls. Then there's the handsome black-and-white motif, ideal lighting, and inviting bar and cocktail menu. Add in inspired coastal Mediterranean cuisine from chef Samuel Peery, who traveled through the south of France dreaming up tempting dishes like chargrilled octopus with bento bacon, three-day cured leeks vinaigrette, and wild boar chops Provençale, and who wants to leave?

MISS RIVER, FRENCH QUARTER

Chef Alon Shaya's love letter to Louisiana offers a spirited take on the local dishes of his adopted city in the beautiful Four Seasons Hotel New Orleans. His wife, Emily's, award-winning red beans and rice is a side, fried chicken is presented whole and then carved tableside, and there is a Gulf red snapper encrusted in salt. Swank touches abound—caviar with Creole cream cheese ice cream, anyone? Forget the budget; this is an experience to indulge.

RESTAURANT R'EVOLUTION, FRENCH QUARTER

More a restaurant in a hotel than a hotel restaurant, this stunner from chefs John Folse and Rick Tramonto opened in The Royal Sonesta New Orleans in 2012. At once a steak house, a modern Italian trattoria, and a polished Creole-Cajun restaurant, R'evolution offers accomplished luxury-grade cooking at its best. Get the signature death by gumbo: a whole roasted quail, andouille, and oysters in a silky broth. Possibly life-changing. One of the best wine cellars in town.

SEAWORTHY, CBD

Seaworthy is in the Ace, but you have to go outside and walk a few steps to enter the classic Creole cottage built in 1832, where an intimate evening of seafood awaits. Try oysters raw and grilled, caviar crudo, snapper collar, or fish and chips made with local fluke, all in a setting that evokes a luxury wooden schooner's cabin.

EMERIL'S

800 Tchoupitoulas Street
emerilsrestaurant.com

A FAMILY LEGACY BURNS BRIGHT

At twenty-one, E. J. Lagasse bears a striking resemblance to his celebrity chef father at the same age. Emeril Lagasse's only son is also the only of his children intent on a culinary career. When E. J. was ten, he told his dad he wanted to be a chef. The response was, if he was sure, he couldn't start his career working for his dad.

Laser focused on his goal, E. J. graduated from Johnson & Wales University's culinary school early and has staged, or interned, at Michelin-starred restaurants in New York, London, and Stockholm. When Emeril's finally reopened after being shuttered for more than a year during the pandemic, E. J. was part of the opening team.

The reimagined Emeril's offered an à la carte menu along with an elevated chef's tasting experience. Changes, both in the restaurant's menu and décor, were in the works pre-pandemic, as the company readied for its thirtieth anniversary. Tim Alvarez joined the team as creative culinary director in February 2020, coming to Emeril's from the Michelin-starred Le Bernardin in New York, where he worked as sous chef for menu development. He arrived a month before the shutdown. Two of the company's local restaurants never reopened—Delmonico and NOLA in the French Quarter. Locals still mourn their loss.

The modern approach to the chef's take on New Orleans cuisine is well illustrated in the presentation of Emeril's iconic banana cream pie, long a towering, exuberant version of the classic dessert. The resulting redo is both elegant and subtle, without losing a smidge of creamy banana goodness—a refined version that would be at home in a fine French patisserie.

While the à la carte menu is offered in the more casual bar side of the restaurant, there is a set-course seasonal menu priced at $175, and a $195 progression through classic, signature dishes delivered with sophisticated polish. New additions include a version of the chef's famous barbecue shrimp and a fish of the day, served with potato mousse, as well as Louisiana Wagyu carpaccio presented with champagne sabayon and a hybrid sturgeon caviar, along with house-made crackers speckled with Tellicherry pepper. A whole grilled and butterflied fish is topped with warm rémoulade that pops with smoked trout roe.

The restaurant's bar and lounge, now called The Salon, offers the likes of gumbo, duck pot-pie, and mussels carbonara, as well as fancier plates of caviar and foie gras. Dining at The Salon is the only way to pick your own dishes; the main dining room is the chefs' domain.

Emeril was just twenty-three when he took over the kitchen at Commander's Palace. He opened Emeril's in a then-rough stretch of the Warehouse Arts District in 1990. Before long, he was a bona fide celebrity chef with a storied television career, a burgeoning restaurant empire, and his own product line. His foundation continues to raise millions of dollars for underserved youth.

While his business mindfully contracted during the pandemic, the celebrity chef's influence remains strong. With his son by his side, a new chapter of the Emeril Lagasse story is unfolding. E. J. is excited to be working with his father, his face animated when he talks about the possibilities. The future is bright.

Chef E. J. Lagasse is crazy about tasso, a spiced Cajun specialty made from boneless pork shoulder that can liven up everything from red beans and rice to shrimp and grits. Slightly fattier than regular ham, tasso adds a rich, smoky depth to this elegant cream sauce. Chef E. J., now in a leading role in his family's restaurant, makes homemade ravioli in the kitchen at Emeril's as part of a classic tasting menu. Guests enjoy a single large raviolo topped with tasso foam, a variation of a dish that's been on the menu since the 1990s. If you don't have time to make the pasta, fresh lasagna sheets, sold in Whole Foods in the cheese section and at most gourmet stores, offer a simple alternative to making ravioli at home.

SERVES 4

RAVIOLI

BASIC PASTA DOUGH (PAGE 146), ROLLED OUT

TASSO SAUCE (PAGE 147)

¾ POUND SHRIMP, PEELED, DEVEINED, AND BLANCHED

2½ TEASPOONS SHRIMP OR CHICKEN STOCK

1 TEASPOON TOMATO PASTE

4 TEASPOONS HOT SAUCE

3 GARLIC CLOVES, ROASTED AND PEELED

¼ CUP HEAVY CREAM

2½ TABLESPOONS CHOPPED PARSLEY

1⅓ CUPS CHOPPED AND BLANCHED LEEKS

½ TEASPOON MINCED SCALLION, WHITE PART ONLY

GRATED ZEST OF ½ LEMON

1 TEASPOON CAYENNE

SEA SALT AND GROUND WHITE PEPPER, TO TASTE

1. Prepare pasta sheets.

2. Prepare Tasso Sauce.

3. In food processor or using immersion blender, blend shrimp with stock, tomato paste, hot sauce, roasted garlic, and heavy cream until smooth.

4. Fold in parsley, leeks, scallion, lemon zest, and cayenne.

5. Adjust seasoning with sea salt and ground white pepper.

6. Using fresh pasta sheets, place teaspoons of filling 2 inches apart and 1 inch from edges. Each sheet should yield about 4 ravioli. Cut in between ravioli and fold pasta over. Press edges with your fingers, removing any air bubbles, and then seal edges with fork.

7. Cook in boiling water 3–4 minutes or until al dente, then drain.

continued...

BASIC PASTA DOUGH

YIELD: 1¾ pounds pasta

4 CUPS ALL-PURPOSE FLOUR,
PLUS MORE AS NEEDED

1 TEASPOON KOSHER SALT

2 LARGE EGGS

8 LARGE EGG YOLKS

1 TABLESPOON EXTRA-VIRGIN
OLIVE OIL

1. In the bowl of food processor, combine flour and salt. Process to mix well. With machine running, add eggs, egg yolks, and olive oil through feed tube, and process until mixture resembles wet cornmeal, about 2 minutes.

2. Take a handful of dough at a time and form into a firm ball. Repeat with remaining dough. Using pasta machine or rolling pin, roll pasta into sheets on lightly floured surface until desired thickness is reached.

TASSO SAUCE

YIELDS 1 QUART

1 TEASPOON NEUTRAL OIL
1 POUND TASSO HAM, CUBED
1 LARGE ONION, SLICED
4 GARLIC CLOVES, SLICED THIN
2 TABLESPOONS MINCED SHALLOT

2½ CUPS WHITE WINE
6½ CUPS MILK
1 TEASPOON FINE SEA SALT
1 TEASPOON CAYENNE

1. Set pan over medium-high heat with just enough neutral oil to coat bottom.

2. Add tasso ham and render a few minutes.

3. Add onion, garlic, and shallot and cook until translucent.

4. Deglaze pan with white wine and simmer until liquid is absorbed.

5. Add milk and continue to simmer, stirring frequently.

6. Add fine sea salt and cayenne.

7. Cook until reduced and thickened, about 15 minutes.

8. Blend with immersion blender until frothy.

9. Divide ravioli into four shallow bowls and top with sauce to serve.

FRITAI

1535 Basin Street
fritai.com

CHANNELING CULINARY PARALLELS BETWEEN
HAITI AND NEW ORLEANS

Diri kole is a staple of Haitian cuisine, a traditional one-pot dish made of rice, red beans, garlic, parsley, and cloves. Like so many Haitian dishes, it's flavored by epis—a blend of spices, garlic, and herbs akin to the Creole and Cajun holy trinity.

If this sounds similar to the New Orleans Monday special, red beans and rice, that's because it is. There is a strong resonance between New Orleans and Haiti, the inspiration for chef Charly Pierre's restaurant, Fritai, on the edge of Treme, the oldest Black neighborhood in America. Charly's parents immigrated to the United States in 1988, settling in Cambridge, Massachusetts, the year before he was born. His father was a chef with Marriott, and his mother cooked homestyle Haitian dishes for the family.

Charly, who went to culinary school and worked in fine dining restaurants in Boston before moving to New Orleans in 2015, is a product of both influences. "New Orleans is deeply connected to Haiti, in so many ways," said the chef.

That connection drills down to the city's roots. After the Haitian Revolution in 1804, an uprising against slavery and French colonizers, some ten thousand immigrants came to New Orleans over the next five years, doubling the city's population. This growth and influx of French Caribbean culture added dimension and depth to an already diverse city. Charly felt a shock of recognition the first time he came to New Orleans. Cities like Port-au-Prince echo the French Quarter's style of architecture. Haitians eat a version of gumbo, cochon de lait, and beignets. This was exactly the place for Charly to open his own Haitian restaurant.

Along with partner Minerva "Eva" Chereches, Charly opened Fritai at the St. Roch Market as a food stall in 2016. The name Fritai means "fried" and refers to the fried snacks that he ate on the street during his regular visits to Haiti to see friends and family.

Charly opened the brick-and-mortar Fritai in 2021. His fans followed, already addicted to the likes of his Fritai sandwich, fried plantains stuffed with rafts of crispy pork, slices of avocado, and spicy mango relish. Named Restaurant of the Year by Eater New Orleans in 2021, the chef was a James Beard Award finalist in 2022.

One of his favorite homey menu items is smoked fish pasta, just called "spaghetti" by Haitians. "We even eat it for breakfast," he said. The popular street food is a sauté of smoked herring with epis and tomato paste, tossed with homemade pasta.

There's a pan-roasted fish, usually red snapper, rubbed with epis and roasted until crispy, with red beans, plantain, and Creole sauce on the side. A simple stewed Creole chicken is kissing cousins to the smothered chicken served by New Orleans home cooks. Spicy wings are flavored with mango and served with an avocado dip. Charly's goal, as he cooks in his busy Treme restaurant, is to showcase his family roots while celebrating the local food culture of New Orleans.

CHILLED WATERMELON AND ROASTED PEPPER SOUP

Cooking on an open fire is a technique that chef Charly associates with his family's Haitian roots, a common way his aunties added the smoky flavors of charred fruits and vegetables into a spectrum of dishes. He remembers his mother using lemon juice to brighten meats and seafood, and charring vegetables to add depth of flavor to a sauce. This refreshing chilled soup, with its lively notes of citrus and spice, brings ingredients together that remind him of both New Orleans and Haiti, two cuisines that are engraved into his culinary DNA.

SERVES 2

2 GREEN BELL PEPPERS

½ SCOTCH BONNET PEPPER

1 LARGE ONION

4 CUPS CUBED WATERMELON

1 TABLESPOON CHOPPED PARSLEY

¼ CUP CRYSTAL HOT SAUCE

3 TABLESPOONS CREOLE SEASONING

½ CUP WHITE WINE VINEGAR

⅓ CUP STEEN'S CANE SYRUP

JUICE AND ZEST OF 2 LIMES

¼ CUP FRESH LEMON JUICE

FRESH CRABMEAT, OPTIONAL

PLANTAIN CHIPS, OPTIONAL

1. On an open flame, roast peppers until skin is completely charred, rotating so that char is even. Immediately place charred peppers in pot or metal bowl with tight-fitting lid. Cover and let stand 10–15 minutes or until peppers are cool enough to handle. Carefully peel away charred skin. Discard. Cut up peppers, removing and discarding ribs and seeds.

2. Peel and cut onion in half and roast over flame until cut surface is blackened. Use knife to pare away any char from onion.

3. In large bowl, combine all ingredients (not the crabmeat and plantain chips) and blend with immersion blender or in traditional blender until semismooth. Chill before serving.

4. Top with fresh crabmeat and plantain chips, if desired.

GRIS-GRIS

1800 Magazine Street
grisgrisnola.com

GRIS-GRIS BRINGS GOOD JUJU TO THE LOWER GARDEN DISTRICT

In 2018, chef Eric Cook opened his flagship restaurant, Gris-Gris, a chic, comfortable eatery and bar in a triangular building in the Lower Garden District. The space came with the bonus of outdoor seating on the deep second-floor balcony. Like Magazine Street itself, Gris-Gris reveals different faces as one moves through the space. Firmly rooted in New Orleans's singular style of warm hospitality, Gris-Gris features inspired takes on the Southern cuisine locals cherish and visitors crave.

"I feel like we are right at the gateway to Magazine Street," said the New Orleans native. "This is where the action starts to pick up. There are people everywhere. It's full of life."

Enter from the street to the option of food-bar seating around the open kitchen. Chef Eric, as engaging as he is talented, is quick with a generous welcome and conversation. Head up the stairs to a collection of wooden tables surrounding an expansive cocktail bar and access to that magical balcony. The second level also affords access to The Samedi Room, Eric's private dining and event space, which includes its own kitchen and dining table for up to twelve people, with the option of seating more. Named for Baron Samedi, a Voodoo loa, or spirit, The Samedi Room has a third-floor private lounge space with plush seating, a large-screen TV, and two additional outdoor balcony spaces over Magazine Street.

Eric should be familiar to those who follow New Orleans culinary news. His twenty-five-year career has included stops in the kitchens of Brennan's, Commander's Palace, Dickie Brennan's Bourbon House, Tommy's Cuisine, and New Orleans Social House (NOSH).

The journey gave him plenty of time to figure out what he wanted to do in his own place. "I'm staying in my lane," Eric said. "I'm doing what I do well and not trying to be everything to everyone."

Expertly fried Gulf oysters make two memorable appearances on the starter menu. They are the main attraction on a refreshing salad with crisp Little Gem lettuce, thin shavings of watermelon radish, a scattering of blue cheese, and a hint of sugarcane vinaigrette. They costar in a fun take on a BLT, alongside cubes of smoked pork belly and a sensational tomato jam. A silken tomato butter sauce elevates the shrimp and fried green tomatoes to game-changing status. Same for the smoked sausage, roasted red peppers, and cherry tomatoes that enhance the shrimp and Gris-Gris grits.

OYSTER AND ARTICHOKE STEW

ouisiana's early European settlers must have been thrilled to find oysters, a common and cherished food in France, plentiful in their new home and a mainstay of the indigenous community's diet. Today, oysters continue to play an important role in the state's culinary culture. Oysters are at their prime in late fall through spring. In this stew, reduced heavy cream imparts the velvety texture, and the richness is counterbalanced by the brightness of the tarragon and the minerality of the charred artichokes. This stew is best made one day in advance, which will also take pressure off if you are preparing for a holiday dinner or gathering. The artichokes can be blackened at the last minute before serving.

2 PINTS SHUCKED OYSTERS IN THEIR LIQUID (AKA OYSTER LIQUOR)

2 TABLESPOONS UNSALTED BUTTER

1 SMALL ONION, FINELY DICED

8 CUPS (2 QUARTS) HEAVY CREAM

1 TABLESPOON CHOPPED TARRAGON

2 TABLESPOONS BLENDED 80% CANOLA /20% OLIVE OIL

1 (14 ½-OUNCE) CAN QUARTERED ARTICHOKE HEARTS, DRAINED AND PATTED DRY

1 TABLESPOON ZATARAIN'S CREOLE SEASONING

¼ CUP VERY THINLY SLICED SCALLIONS, GREEN PARTS ONLY

KOSHER SALT AND BLACK PEPPER, TO TASTE

SERVES 6-8

1. Drain oysters over bowl to catch oyster liquor. Refrigerate oysters, but keep oyster liquor at hand.

continued...

2. Add butter to 3- or 4-quart heavy saucepan, preferably cast-iron Dutch oven, over medium-low heat. Add onion and sweat, stirring constantly until translucent, 3–5 minutes. Do not allow onion to brown.

3. Add heavy cream, reserved oyster liquor, and tarragon to pot. Watch carefully to not scorch cream. When mixture comes to slight boil, about 10 minutes, reduce heat to low and simmer, whisking occasionally, until cream has thickened and reduced by 25 percent, about 1 hour.

4. If you are preparing stew one day in advance (and you really should), allow stew to cool, then refrigerate until a half hour before serving time. Gently reheat stew over low heat until it is simmering, 15–20 minutes.

5. Add 1 tablespoon blended oil to well-seasoned cast-iron pan. Spread oil with paper towel to leave thin coating in pan, and set oiled pan over medium-high heat.

6. Add drained artichokes to bowl. Add remaining tablespoon oil and Creole seasoning, and toss gently to thoroughly coat artichokes.

7. Arrange artichokes in single layer in hot pan and cook until charred, 2–3 minutes. Turn artichokes and char other side. Remove from heat and set aside.

8. Remove reserved oysters from refrigerator. When stew has come to simmer, add scallions and reserved oysters, and cook until oysters plump and edges curl, 2–3 minutes.

9. Taste stew and add salt and pepper as needed.

10. Ladle stew into shallow soup plates. Divide blackened artichokes among each portion and serve immediately.

GW FINS

808 Bienville Street
gwfins.com

CHEF MICHAEL NELSON BLAZES A SEAFOOD TRAIL

Michael Nelson's world is defined by water.

As executive chef at the award-winning GW Fins in New Orleans, Michael depends on the lakes and the estuaries, rivers, and bayous that feed into the Gulf to supply the restaurant's seafood bounty. But beyond just the simplicity of delicious local seafood, Michael is obsessed with sustainability, commissioning local spear fishermen and using bycatch and invasive fish to create a groundbreaking menu.

For the past decade, Michael, a nationally recognized expert on Gulf seafood, has dealt exclusively with whole fish. "I realized that only 23 to 45 percent of a fish was being used. The rest was going into the garbage. It would be like cutting the breasts off a chicken and throwing the rest away." Although it takes more space, time, and manpower to break down a whole fish, the result is worth it, he said.

By butchering fish in-house, he's able to utilize parts like the flavorful belly and the collar around the neck and throat, raising his yield as high as 60 percent for redfish, for example. "That's 40 percent more than we were getting." His tempura fried fish "wings" served with a sweet, spicy Korean glaze are a case in point: tender white meat with a fin "handle" that utilizes what used to be waste. "We take the wings off every fish that we can—drum, sheepshead, red snapper. It's one of our most popular menu items."

Michael is the kind of chef who is always thinking, pushing boundaries. Take his dry-aging program, for example. He figured, if it works for beef, maybe it can transform tuna and swordfish into something new. The James Beard Award–nominated chef had dry-aging lockers adapted for prime cuts of fish, programmed to keep an exact temperature and humidity level while the air inside is circulated through UV light. The key is starting with the freshest fish caught in the past twenty-four hours or so. The process radically improves the texture and flavor of fish, creating a new kind of seafood umami.

Another of Michael's finny projects is swapping out seafood for the usual cured meats on charcuterie platters; think sea-cuterie made from every part of the 700–1,000 pounds of fish that's butchered in-house daily. Tuna and swordfish translate to smoked kielbasa and andouille sausage, pepperoni, and bacon. Even the skins are transformed into crispy fish cracklins.

"There is nothing more exhilarating than working with fresh seafood," said the Chicago native, who has been in the GW Fins kitchen for close to two decades. "We like to say that nature writes our menu, because it changes every afternoon, based on the ingredients that come through our doors that day. That sense of anticipation, of creativity in our kitchen, is something that I thrive on."

BARBECUE GULF SHRIMP

Barbecue shrimp is a quintessential New Orleans seafood dish, although the name can be a puzzler for those new to the specialty. The shrimp is not barbecued at all; instead, it's bathed in a buttery, Worcestershire-fueled sauce that is just made for mopping up with crusty bread. At GW Fins, chef Michael insists on seafood that was recently swimming in the Gulf, which takes this dish to an ethereal level. Prepare the Barbecue Shrimp Butter in advance and keep it in the freezer. Just add shrimp fresh off the boat to the defrosted butter, and a restaurant-quality meal is on the table in a matter of minutes.

SERVES 6-8

1 POUND FRESH HEAD-ON LOUISIANA SHRIMP (10–15 COUNT OR BIGGER)

¾ TEASPOON CHEF PAUL PRUDHOMME SHRIMP MAGIC OR CREOLE SEASONING

1 TABLESPOON UNSALTED BUTTER

1 TABLESPOON EXTRA-VIRGIN OLIVE OIL

3 OUNCES ABITA AMBER (YOU'LL HAVE HALF A BOTTLE LEFT OVER FOR DRINKING)

¼ POUND COLD BARBECUE SHRIMP BUTTER (PAGE 162)

1 TABLESPOON CHOPPED PARSLEY

FRENCH OR SOURDOUGH BREAD, FOR DIPPING (OR MASHED POTATOES)

1. Peel shrimp, leaving heads attached; split each shrimp back ¼ inch and remove sand vein.

2. Season with Shrimp Magic or Creole seasoning.

3. In large skillet, heat butter and olive oil over medium-high heat. Add seasoned shrimp and sauté 2 minutes. Flip and continue cooking 1 minute.

4. Add beer and reduce by half.

5. Lower heat and stir in several chunks of Barbecue Shrimp Butter.

6. Continue adding butter, stirring constantly to make sauce a creamy consistency. Add parsley.

7. Serve in large, preheated bowls, with plenty of bread for dipping or over mashed potatoes.

continued...

BARBECUE SHRIMP BUTTER

1 POUND, PLUS ¼ CUP UNSALTED BUTTER

6 TABLESPOONS FINELY DICED SHALLOTS

6 TABLESPOONS FINELY DICED GARLIC

2 TABLESPOONS FRESH LEMON JUICE

2 TABLESPOONS REDUCED VEAL OR CHICKEN STOCK (OPTIONAL)

2 TABLESPOONS CHOPPED ROSEMARY

1 TABLESPOON PAPRIKA

1½ TEASPOONS CHOPPED THYME

1½ TEASPOONS BLACK PEPPER

1½ TEASPOONS KOSHER SALT

1 PINCH CAYENNE

1 TEASPOON WORCESTERSHIRE SAUCE

1. Melt ¼ cup butter in small, heavy-bottomed saucepan.

2. Place diced shallots and garlic in butter and cook over low to medium heat, covered, until soft but not browned. Spread mixture on sheet pan and refrigerate until cold.

3. Place 1 pound butter in stand mixer with paddle and whip on high until white and fluffy.

4. Reduce speed and add remaining ingredients, as well as refrigerated shallot-and-garlic mixture.

5. Increase speed and whip 1 minute on high. Roll up mixture in plastic wrap into log that is 2 inches in diameter. Refrigerate or freeze until needed. Can be frozen for up to 2 months.

HERBSAINT

701 St. Charles Avenue
herbsaint.com

A FLAGSHIP RESTAURANT CHARTS A CHEF'S JOURNEY

Herbsaint is a restaurant with a distinct sense of place. Between the St. Charles Avenue streetcar rumbling just steps from its front door and a menu that charts the nexus of rustic Creole, French, and Italian cuisine, Herbsaint is clearly a New Orleans original.

The restaurant is named for the anise-flavored liqueur birthed in New Orleans, which is as notable for flavoring dishes like oysters Rockefeller as it is for being an essential ingredient in cocktails like the classic Sazerac. Donald Link opened Herbsaint in 2000 as a partnership with chef Susan Spicer. The pair had worked together when Donald was a sous chef at Bayona. He bought Susan out of the business a few years after Katrina. In 2007, the restaurant earned chef Donald a James Beard Award for Best Chef: South, just the first in the string of accolades and awards that have followed his career, which is heading into its fourth decade.

Born in Roberts Cove near Rayne, Louisiana, Donald grew up in Lake Charles and learned his love of rustic Cajun cooking and seasonal ingredients from his grandparents. He got his first restaurant job at fifteen but opted to study finance in college. It wasn't until he was twenty-three that he decided cooking was going to be his life. Donald went to culinary school in California, then worked at and opened fine restaurants in the Bay Area before returning to New Orleans to open Herbsaint, the first but not the last love letter to his adopted city.

Herbsaint's menu, while refined, is shot through with a Louisiana Cajun accent, from local citrus to house-made tasso and andouille. The cooking defies categorization, yet it's always intriguing, always consistent. Louisiana shrimp may arrive bathed in coconut curry; duck confit comes with a side of dirty rice. Fried apple hand pies vie with pot de crème for dessert. Herbsaint is the chef's flagship, and with good reason.

Donald has grown his business mindfully. He's a man of his word, with a reputation for a collaborative management style, qualities he shares with business partner Stephen Stryjewski. The Link Restaurant Group (LRG) has opened some of the most important restaurants in New Orleans, including Cochon, Cochon Butcher, Pêche Seafood Grill, La Boulangerie, and Gianna. His latest project, Chemin à la Mer (French for "pathway to the sea"), a swank French steak and seafood restaurant with spectacular views of the Mississippi, opened in November 2022 in the Four Seasons Hotel New Orleans.

At this stage in his career, with a lifetime of restaurant experience under his belt, Donald doesn't have a thing to prove to anybody. He's won the awards, written the books, traveled the charity and festival circuits, started a foundation, and grown a company that endured during the toughest of times. "What I really care about now is just making good food. The creativity, the sport of it. That's what matters to me."

DUCK AND ANDOUILLE GUMBO

James Beard Award–winning chef Donald flexes his Cajun muscles with this zesty gumbo recipe, with its oh-so-slight hint of heat. The chef comes by his propensity for spice honestly; schooled in Southern and Cajun cuisine by his grandparents, chef Donald loves this recipe for its connection to the culture of South Louisiana, where duck hunting is a favored activity and andouille sausage a birthright.

SERVES 6-8

1 4- TO 5-POUND DUCK

1 TABLESPOON PLUS 2 TEASPOONS KOSHER SALT

2½ TEASPOONS BLACK PEPPER

2 CUPS ALL-PURPOSE FLOUR

1¼ CUPS VEGETABLE OIL

1 MEDIUM ONION, SMALL DICED

3 STALKS CELERY, SMALL DICED

1 POBLANO PEPPER, SMALL DICED

1 GREEN BELL PEPPER, SMALL DICED

1 JALAPEÑO, FINELY CHOPPED

3 GARLIC CLOVES, MINCED

1½ TEASPOONS CHILI POWDER

1½ TEASPOONS FILÉ POWDER

1 TEASPOON CAYENNE

1 TEASPOON WHITE PEPPER

1 TEASPOON PAPRIKA

3 QUARTS CHICKEN STOCK

1 POUND ANDOUILLE SAUSAGE, SLICED INTO ½-INCH HALF-MOONS

2 CUPS CHOPPED OKRA (OPTIONAL)

COOKED WHITE RICE, FOR SERVING

CHOPPED SCALLIONS, FOR GARNISH

continued

1. Cut duck in 8–10 pieces. Remove skin (reserve if you feel like making cracklins), but leave bones in. Season duck with 2 teaspoons salt and 1 teaspoon black pepper. Coat duck with ½ cup flour, shaking off excess.

2. Add oil to large, heavy pot, preferably cast-iron Dutch oven, over medium-high heat.

3. Pan-fry duck pieces in oil until lightly golden. Remove from pot and set aside.

4. Reduce heat to medium. To remaining oil, add 1½ cups flour and stir constantly with wooden spoon over medium heat until deep-brown roux is achieved, 20–30 minutes.

5. Add vegetables and seasonings and stir to combine.

6. Add chicken stock and pan-fried duck pieces. Increase heat to high and bring to boil. Take care to stir gumbo occasionally as it comes to boil, so roux does not stick to bottom.

7. As soon as gumbo comes to boil, reduce heat to low and simmer 50 minutes, occasionally skimming oil from top.

8. Add andouille and simmer until duck meat begins to fall off the bone, another 30–45 minutes.

9. If using okra in your gumbo, add it now; make sure to quick sauté first to get some of the sliminess out. Serve each bowl with a tablespoon of rice, or to taste, and garnish with some chopped scallions.

JACK ROSE

2031 St. Charles Avenue
jackroserestaurant.com

A CLASSIC REINVIGORATED

Jack Rose is a party waiting to happen, a celebratory space oozing color, style, and pop-culture chic. In 2018, the restaurant took over the former Caribbean Room, long a stalwart dining experience in the storied Pontchartrain Hotel on St. Charles Avenue. Somehow, it just didn't work in the newly renovated hotel, which opened under its original name in 2016.

Out with the fusty, in with the lusty. It's no coincidence that co-owner/chef Brian Landry was at the helm of Galatoire's for years. He knows how to set the scene for a good time, as is the tradition for Friday lunch at that Creole icon on Bourbon Street.

Jack Rose marked the debut for QED Hospitality, a company created by partners Landry and Emery Whalen, longtime hospitality managers who joined forces in late 2017. They run all of the hotel's food and beverage, along with projects in Nashville and a restaurant in a Kentucky bourbon distillery.

Chef Brian is a New Orleans native known for his dedication to conserving Gulf seafood and regional foodways. As for the restaurant's name, it's inspired by the Tennessee Williams play *The Rose Tattoo*. Williams was living at the Pontchartrain when he wrote *A Streetcar Named Desire*, just one of the many stories about the famous hotel.

Part of Jack Rose's liveliness stems from the way the restaurant's space is configured. Guests can wander through an art-filled lounge punctuated by brightly colored groups of sofas and chairs. A rose-lined patio and multiple dining rooms are all ready to serve bubbles and small plates or platters heaped with Chianti-braised short ribs and local fish en papillote with crab boil butter–crisped fingerling potatoes on the side. The menu is contemporary and playful, with copious local references—a mix of craveable Italian, French, and Spanish dishes created with plenty of New Orleans verve.

A favorite dish is fried chicken parmesan, the quintessential Sicilian-Creole hybrid served on the bone. Beyond the crackle of the fried bird is the brilliant addition of red gravy and melted mozzarella cheese. The veal chop is a riff on saltimbocca, with the bone-in chop subbing for the paneed cutlet, adorned with slivers of prosciutto and fried sage.

One thing that will never come off the menu is the Mile High Pie, a tower of tricolor ice cream that brings out the kid in anybody. The skyscraper confection is made of layers of chocolate, vanilla, and peppermint ice cream, topped with gooey meringue and a river of dark-chocolate sauce poured tableside.

Thankfully some food memories are alive and well at Jack Rose in the Pontchartrain Hotel. And so many others are still in the making.

MILE HIGH PIE

Serving towering wedges of Mile High Pie is chef Brian's way of paying homage to the famed Caribbean Room, the long-standing restaurant in the Pontchartrain Hotel where Jack Rose is now. The original pie was created by Black pastry chef Annie Laura Squalls, who became head baker at the Caribbean Room in 1960. Her pie is still the number-one dessert order at Jack Rose, keeping this relatively unknown pastry chef's legacy alive. Note that you'll need one medium stainless-steel ice bucket to re-create it in your own home.

SERVES 10-12

1 QUART PEPPERMINT ICE CREAM

1 QUART VANILLA ICE CREAM

1 QUART CHOCOLATE ICE CREAM

1 CHOCOLATE COOKIE PIECRUST

MERINGUE

8 LARGE EGG WHITES

½ TEASPOON VANILLA EXTRACT

½ TEASPOON CREAM OF TARTAR

½ CUP SUGAR

1 (11¾-OUNCE) JAR CHOCOLATE SAUCE, FOR SERVING

1. In bowl, use rubber spatula to mix peppermint ice cream until it's the consistency of soft-serve ice cream.

2. Place peppermint ice cream in ice bucket, being sure to smooth out ice cream as much as possible. Place in freezer about an hour or until set.

3. Place vanilla ice cream in another bowl and mix to soft-serve consistency, then layer on top of peppermint ice cream. Let vanilla ice cream freeze about an hour or until set.

continued...

4. Repeat same steps with chocolate ice cream, layering onto vanilla and allowing to freeze.

5. Crumble cookie piecrust and sprinkle generously on top of chocolate ice cream. Using bottom of water glass, press cookie crumble into chocolate ice cream, making sure layer is dense enough to hold pie when inverted.

6. Freeze entire pie 2 hours or until ice cream is set.

7. Remove from freezer, place serving plate upside down on top of ice bucket, and invert. Using your hands (or small blowtorch), warm ice bucket and shake gently to remove ice cream. If pie is resistant, try placing skewer inside center of ice cream to help release.

Make Meringue:

1. In large bowl, beat egg whites with vanilla and cream of tartar until soft peaks form.

2. Gradually add sugar, beating until egg whites are stiff and glossy and sugar is dissolved.

3. Spread meringue over ice cream, using spatula, or add to pastry bag with star tip and pipe onto pie.

4. Toast meringue with small blowtorch.

5. Slice and serve with generous drizzle of chocolate sauce.

JOHNNY SÁNCHEZ

930 Poydras Street
johnnysancheznola.com

CHEF AARÓN SÁNCHEZ TREASURES TIES TO NEW ORLEANS

In his 2019 memoir, *Where I Come From: Life Lessons from a Latino Chef*, Aarón Sánchez offers a deeply personal look back at his career, influences, and passion for both traditional and Nuevo Latino cuisine.

It's a backstory that makes his modern Mexican restaurant, Johnny Sánchez, in the Central Business District, especially notable to New Orleanians. Because it was in New Orleans—as an intern at K-Paul's Louisiana Kitchen—that he came under the tutelage of the late great chef Paul Prudhomme, who conveyed lessons on both life and gastronomy in equal measure. Aarón credits both Prudhomme and Aarón's mother, well-known Mexican chef Zarela Martínez, for shaping him into the man, and chef, he is today.

Aarón grew up in El Paso, Texas, helping his divorced mom with her catering gigs. His mother took a class from Prudhomme early in her career, an experience that shaped both her and her son's life. The renowned Cajun chef urged her to move to New York, where she opened her game-changing restaurant, Zarela, in 1987. When her son started acting up, she sent him to her mentor for some direction.

In his book, Aarón recalls "getting a culinary crash course" at K-Paul's, where "I learned to cook...but he also taught me how to taste."

Although he's often on the road, Aarón considers New Orleans home base. It's where he opened Johnny Sánchez with then partner John Besh in 2014. The two chefs were competitors on the Food Network's *The Next Iron Chef* in 2007 and became friends. Besh left the business, replaced by other partners, in 2018. In 2023, Aarón opened another Johnny Sánchez, this time at L'Auberge Casino Resort in Lake Charles, the same year his breakfast-sandwich restaurant, ShowBird, opened in downtown New Orleans.

A regular on a slew of cooking and travel reality shows, some geared specifically to the Latin market, Aarón is a charismatic natural in front of the camera. His success isn't something he takes lightly. He remembers well the need for purpose and direction as a young man and is intent on uplifting Latino youth.

In 2016, the chef started the philanthropy initiative that would become the Aarón Sánchez Impact Fund in 2022, to provide culinary arts education, mentorship, and human services to empower Latino youth. As of 2023, the program awarded more than $1 million in scholarships, including culinary school tuition, housing, travel and living expenses, and mentorship from Aarón and other culinary professionals.

Although chef/partner Miles Landrem leads the Johnny Sánchez kitchen day-to-day, Aarón is still involved in the restaurant's menu and concept. The albondigas tacos are filled with his grandmother's mint-flecked meatballs, and topped with chipotle gravy, chili mayo, pickled onion, and cotija. Many dishes are conjured from his childhood and travels.

As chef Aarón continues to expand his reach, both in and outside of Louisiana, his sense of home, of connection to both Mexico and New Orleans, remains a driving force.

ARROZ CON POLLO

This is chef Aarón's take on arroz con pollo, rice with chicken. There are myriad ways to prepare this classic dish, served throughout Spain and Latin America, with the ultimate goal of serving a taste of home, comfort on a plate. At Johnny Sánchez, the emphasis is on depth of flavor and texture, which comes from the way the chef cooks the rice. Crispy Rice completely transforms the mouthfeel, making this a memorable version of the classic.

SERVES 4

2 TABLESPOONS COLD UNSALTED BUTTER

1 MEDIUM ONION, JULIENNED OR SLICED

1 POBLANO PEPPER, ROASTED, PEELED, AND CUT IN STRIPS

1 RIPE TOMATO, ROASTED, OR 1 CUP CANNED WHOLE TOMATOES

4 BONELESS CHICKEN THIGHS, GRILLED AND SLICED

½ CUP GOOD-QUALITY RED SALSA

½ CUP CHICKEN OR BEEF STOCK

2 TEASPOONS SEA SALT, PLUS MORE TO TASTE

1 TEASPOON BLACK PEPPER, PLUS MORE TO TASTE

1½ CUPS CRISPY RICE (PAGE 180)

1 AVOCADO, SLICED, FOR GARNISH

1 CUP QUESO FRESCO, FOR GARNISH

1 TEASPOON CHOPPED CILANTRO, FOR GARNISH

1 JALAPEÑO, SEEDED AND SLICED, FOR GARNISH

1 TEASPOON CHOPPED CHIVES OR SCALLION, FOR GARNISH

2 TABLESPOONS EXTRA-VIRGIN OLIVE, FOR GARNISH

1. Add 1 tablespoon butter to sauté pan over medium heat. Once melted and bubbling, add onion and sauté 3–4 minutes, then add roasted poblano and tomato to pan; sauté mixture about 2 minutes.

continued

2. Add sliced grilled chicken, salsa, and stock to pan. Simmer 2–3 minutes until stock is slightly reduced.

3. Add remaining tablespoon butter, stirring into sauce until fully incorporated.

4. Season with salt and pepper and then toss in Crispy Rice, stirring until evenly mixed and rice has absorbed most liquid in pan; mixture should not be too dry or too wet.

5. Plate rice in large bowl and garnish with avocado, queso fresco, salt, and pepper, and finish whole dish with cilantro, sliced jalapeño, chives or scallion, and extra-virgin olive oil.

CRISPY RICE

1½ CUPS PARBOILED RICE

2 CUPS RICE FLOUR

VEGETABLE OIL, AS NEEDED, FOR FRYING

1. Follow directions on package for cooking parboiled rice.

2. When rice is cooked, spread onto sheet pan and let cool in refrigerator.

3. Once cooled, in large bowl toss rice with rice flour well; shake bowl to remove excess flour before frying.

4. Heat 2 inches of oil in deep frying pan. Fry rice in batches until brown and crispy. Don't crowd pan. Set aside.

LE CHAT NOIR

715 St. Charles Avenue

FARM-FRESH CUISINE WORTHY OF THE SPOTLIGHT

At Le Chat Noir, an old theater turned modern restaurant on St. Charles Avenue, chef Seth Temple works wonders with Hakurei turnips, sautéing the small, crunchy vegetable, greens attached, in a miso-fueled umami sauce studded with candied kumquats and fronds of bronze fennel. The result is addictive.

Seth is inspired by Dan Barber's veggie-forward approach to food at Blue Hill at Stone Barns in the Hudson Valley. His menu is about 70 percent locally sourced, with at least half of the dishes either vegan or vegetarian. A wood-fired oven in the open kitchen is situated where the former theater's stage used to be.

A native of Lake Charles, Seth went to the Chef John Folse Culinary Institute, where he earned a scholarship to the Institut Paul Bocuse in France. He cooked in New Orleans at kitchens including Kenton's and Couvant before working at Lyle's, a Michelin-starred restaurant in London.

James Reuter, who founded the breakfast and lunch spot Bearcat Café, opened Le Chat Noir in December 2021. It's an ideal stage for Seth's intentional American cuisine.

The chef cultivates connections with local purveyors like Mushroom Maggie's Farm in West Feliciana Parish and works closely with JV Foods (out of Kenner), a food distribution company that sources from producers including Two Dog Farms in Flora, Mississippi, and Saxon Becnel & Sons citrus in Belle Chasse, Louisiana.

Oysters are harvested primarily from Louisiana and Alabama Gulf waters, with suppliers like Bright Side Oysters out of Grand Isle, Louisiana, farming the bivalves sustainably.

The chef and his team regularly break down whole animals, including heritage pork that they get in two to three times a month from a fifth-generation farmer in Baton Rouge.

The menu's large plates include roast pork served with radicchio and crispy shallots and crab fat agnolotti, tender pasta stuffed with scallop, and crab mousseline topped with poached oysters in an Herbsaint cream sauce. There are perfectly crisped fingerling potatoes, anchovy-lined slices of focaccia, and pearls of Öra King salmon crudo laced with gochujang and dill.

The restaurant's food-friendly wine program is globally accented, with a changing menu of wines by the glass that might include a minerally white from Santorini, Greece, and a fruit-forward Cab Franc from the Bourgueil area of the Loire Valley.

Despite his experience in a Michelin-starred restaurant, Seth is not about using tweezers to compose a formal plate. Instead, he wants his food to be approachable and full of flavor.

Although he's committed to sourcing locally, the last thing he's trying to do is reinvent New Orleans standards. "New Orleanians love their fried and smothered dishes," he said. "We are just taking a different approach."

ROASTED HAKUREI TURNIPS WITH GREENS AND CANDIED KUMQUATS

It's easy to fall madly in love with the humble Hakurei turnip. This little gem of a root vegetable is all about balance, with its sweet, crunchy texture, almost fruity flavor, and slight backbeat of bitterness. Twirl the turnips like linguine, being sure to get citrus in every bite. The depth of clean flavor is worth a standing ovation. Leftover kumquat liquid can be stored in an airtight container in the refrigerator for at least a month. Use the kumquat-infused simple syrup as a cocktail ingredient or as a flavorful substitute for sugar or maple syrup in a salad dressing.

SERVES 2

ROASTED HAKUREI TURNIPS

8 2-INCH HAKUREI OR SCARLET TURNIPS, HALVED, WITH GREENS STILL ATTACHED

½ CUP MISO DRESSING (PAGE 186)

¼ CUP FENNEL FRONDS, FOR GARNISH

CANDIED KUMQUATS, FOR GARNISH (PAGE 187)

1. Preheat oven to 450°F.

2. Rinse turnips thoroughly in ice bath. As a root vegetable, turnips are typically very dirty, so be sure to rinse well.

3. Preheat dry cast-iron skillet in hot oven. Place turnips in pan and roast until al dente, about 10 minutes. Vegetables will be nicely charred and greens crispy. Remove from heat.

4. Place turnips in medium bowl and toss with Miso Dressing, adding more to taste.

5. Divide turnips between 2 plates and garnish with fennel fronds and 10–15 Candied Kumquat halves.

continued...

MISO DRESSING

YIELDS 4 CUPS

¼ CUP GRATED GINGER

¼ CUP GRATED GARLIC

2½ CUPS RED MISO

1¼ CUPS SAMBAL

¾ CUP ORANGE JUICE

¼ CUP FRESH LEMON JUICE

¼ CUP FRESH LIME JUICE

¾ CUP CANDIED KUMQUAT LIQUID

¼ CUP GRAPE-SEED OIL

1. Add ginger and garlic to bowl.

2. Add miso and sambal and create paste.

3. Add citrus juices and kumquat liquid to paste.

4. Whisk grape-seed oil in to emulsify to a dressing consistency. If dressing seems thick, add a little water.

CANDIED KUMQUATS

YIELDS 3 CUPS

2 CUPS SUGAR

1 CUP WATER

1 STICK CINNAMON

20 KUMQUATS, HALVED
AND SEEDED

1. Place sugar, water, and cinnamon in 2-quart pot and heat until sugar is completely dissolved.

2. Remove from heat and add kumquats. Cool to room temperature. Reserve liquid for Miso Dressing and store Candied Kumquats in airtight container in refrigerator.

PLANT-BASED PLACES FOR ALL

New Orleans eaters are famously carnivorous. Meat, especially pork, is a driver for so many iconic dishes, from gumbo to red beans and rice. But things have changed in the past decade. Instead of having to settle for a blah plate of grilled veggies, plant-based eaters in NOLA now have a ton of options, including some spots that tweak comfort-food staples to embrace vegan ingredients, with tasty results. Many restaurants offer plant-based along with meat options—Sneaky Pickle in Bywater and Carmo in the Warehouse Arts District are two—but these six cafés focus only on plant-based and vegetarian dishes.

BREADS ON OAK, UPTOWN

Besides amazing vegan baked goods (cinnamon rolls!), the 100 percent plant-based Breads on Oak dishes savories including a TLTA: tempe, lettuce, tomato, and avocado sandwich; an Impossible burger; and avocado toast on wonderful house bread.

BOTANICALS NOLA, BYWATER

This sunny vegan smoothie and juice bar in Bywater will spike your drink with the likes of sea moss and detox herbs. Try snacks like vegan Belgian waffles, a swell chickpea salad sandwich, and vegan baked goods, including king cake during Carnival season.

I-TAL GARDEN, TREME

I-tal is a family-owned, friendly place serving craveable soul-food dishes like dairy-free mac and cheese and barbecue crispy cauli-wings. The Ra pasta is a winner: smoked jackfruit and grilled veggies bathed in coconut milk atop penne and crispy oyster mushrooms.

ORIGINAL THOUGHT FOOD TRUCK, SEVENTH WARD

Tucked away on Agriculture Street, Original Thought is powered by chef Bolingo Ashay and his wife, Maranda's, commitment to healthy eating and plant fuel. Try their cheesy-style polenta grits, smoked barbecue "pulled" jackfruit, and signature fried buffalo oyster mushroom sandwich.

SWEET SOULFOOD, TREME

Chetwan Sweetlove Smith wants her customers to have the familiar comfort foods they love. But her Creole-inspired homey menu swaps out meat for seitan and vegetables in dishes like jambalaya, stuffed bell peppers, and grillades and grits. Don't forget dessert, including treats like sweet potato pie and bread pudding.

UNDERGROWTH COFFEE, UPTOWN

This proudly queer-owned coffee café holds to a mission statement of kindness, to themselves as owners, their customers, their employees, and the environment. Chef Rylynn Murphy is Undergrowth's head chef and coffee roaster, creating vegetarian and vegan dishes that are welcoming to all. She also makes the café's oat and almond milk, nourishing enough for a spa treatment. Rylynn, a trans woman, and her partners, Alyssa Johnson and Zack Rescoe, are close friends working in a business they love. The all-day menu includes avocado toast drizzled with cashew crème fraîche and arugula on rafts of Leo's sourdough and a seasonal citrus salad made with vegan mozz or goat cheese crumbles on a bed of spring mix, orange segments, and the crunch of agave-roasted cashews. They roast their own coffee and sell it by the pound too.

LENGUA MADRE

1245 Constance Street
lenguamadrenola.com

RECONNECTING WITH JOY IN A KITCHEN WHERE KINDNESS MATTERS

When chef Ana Castro of Lengua Madre made the short list for the James Beard Award for Best Chef: South in 2023, the recognition was sweet indeed. Because Lengua Madre, which means "mother tongue," almost didn't happen.

Born in Texas and raised in Mexico City, Ana first learned the art and joy of cooking from her grandmother. The chef trained at Le Cordon Bleu and worked in fine dining restaurants in Manhattan, including the now-shuttered Michelin-starred Betony.

Yet when she started working in kitchens, she found toxic cultures that sucked the joy out of her work. Ana packed her things and came to see her sister, Lydia, in New Orleans, ready to leave the industry altogether.

It was Lydia who convinced her to give her passion one more try. Ana landed a job as a line cook at Coquette, working for Michael Stoltzfus. While there, she was a finalist for the James Beard Foundation's 2018 Rising Star Award and, in the same year, a recipient of the coveted Ment'or Grant, which allowed her to work for three months under chef Jonathan Tam at Relae, the legendary Copenhagen restaurant that closed in 2020.

Ana moved on to sous chef at Stoltzfus's Italian restaurant, Thalia, and when it closed, it was Stoltzfus who suggested they partner so she could channel modern Mexican cuisine her way. Ana had never worked at a Mexican restaurant before. In New Orleans, supported by a laid-back community of peers and close proximity to her sister, Ana found her center in the kitchen once again and opened Lengua Madre in 2022.

The accolades were fast and furious, including landing on *Bon Appétit*'s 50 Best New Restaurants of 2022, and becoming a 2022 semifinalist for the James Beard Foundation's Best New Restaurant award. She runs her kitchen as an egalitarian community, rejecting the traditional French brigade system in favor of her own model that puts people first and emphasizes collaboration.

It's a formula that is working. Her restaurant offers a nightly five-course menu, a wine list built around vineyards from Spanish-speaking countries, and a bar program that is almost entirely of Mexican provenance. The groovy lounge-meets-dining space is awash in pink neon and local art, with seating for thirty-six. Service is expert and warm, and there's a team approach to introducing dishes on the changing menu that unfolds as a surprise over the course of the meal.

One evening, dinner started with a warm shot of shrimp broth, a flavor-packed slurp built on slowly steeped shells and heads, citrus, and a hint of heat on the back end. The broth was presented on a bed of dried black beans, rice, and corn—three ingredients that inform many of the restaurant's dishes. A white mole studded with puffed amaranth, an ancient grain that predates colonization, is topped with fried cauliflower. There's crispy roasted pork-belly pibil, served with x'nipec spicy sauce, a Yucatan specialty made with habanero peppers, with warm house tortillas on the side.

While Ana doesn't believe it's possible to re-create childhood flavors or dishes exactly, she feels her grandmother with her, always. "I try to have my grandmother represented in some way in everything that I do."

Chef Ana is opening Acamaya, specializing in coastal Mexican cuisine, in the spring of 2024 in Bywater.

GULF SHRIMP, HAMACHI, AND CLAM AGUACHILE

You can serve this delicious aguachile with any fresh Louisiana seafood. In this version, chef Ana features shrimp, clams, and pristine hamachi, but you can also use red snapper, crabmeat, or whatever is fresh and readily available. The lime juice "cooks" the seafood, but if you prefer, you can poach the shrimp before using and add it to the finished dish.

SERVES 4-6

12 GULF SHRIMP, PEELED AND DEVEINED

½ POUND HAMACHI, THINLY SLICED

4–6 LIMES, PLUS ½ CUP FRESH LIME JUICE

1 CAN LITTLENECK OR RAZOR CLAMS IN BRINE, DRAINED

1 CUCUMBER

6 TOMATILLOS, HUSKED AND RINSED

2 STALKS CELERY, WITH LEAVES

1 SERRANO PEPPER, STEMMED

1 BUNCH CILANTRO

KOSHER SALT, TO TASTE

1 RED ONION, VERY THINLY SLICED, FOR GARNISH

TORTILLA CHIPS, FOR SERVING

1. In large bowl, combine shrimp and hamachi with ½ cup lime juice. Let sit about 20 minutes, then drain and discard juice. If using razor clams, cut them into bite-size pieces.

2. Peel and seed cucumber. Roughly chop cucumber with tomatillos, celery, serrano, and cilantro, and add to blender. Puree until smooth, then strain through fine-mesh sieve.

3. Season aguachile with juice of 4 limes and salt to taste. Add more lime juice for a brighter and tarter mixture, if you like.

4. To serve, place shrimp, hamachi, and clams in serving bowl or wide, shallow individual bowls and pour aguachile around them. Garnish with shaved red onion and serve with tortilla chips.

LUVI

5236 Tchoupitoulas Street
luvirestaurant.com

CHEF HAO GONG MAKES IT PERSONAL

If LUVI chef Hao Gong ever decides to change careers, he might consider becoming a surgeon. Or maybe a pilot. To say the man is detail oriented and meticulous is like saying Mardi Gras is a party. There's not a wasted move in his kitchen. Hao's precisely executed Chinese and Japanese cuisine is a wonder to behold, but just wait until you taste it.

Opened in a former Uptown donut shop in 2018, LUVI is Hao's first restaurant. But he's been training to be his own boss for years. Hao, a Shanghai native, went to culinary school in China before immigrating to the States, where he first worked in Japanese restaurants in California. After moving to New Orleans, he headed the kitchen at Sake Café before opening LUVI.

His restaurant is a family affair. It's named for daughters Lulu and Violet. And his wife, Jennifer Wade, transformed the compact double shotgun on Tchoupitoulas into a bright, inviting space. The interior is striking, with turquoise walls, floral-printed chairs, and graphic references to both Japanese and Chinese cultures. The bespoke wooden chef's bar from NOLA Boards offers the best up-close chance to watch Hao turn raw fish into edible art.

The Feed Me menu puts guests in Hao's hands, a three-course all-raw menu that brings eye-popping seafood to the plate. This isn't the place to get a dragon roll topped with spicy mayo. But there is a raw bar, where Hao makes tidbits like monkey snack: sesame-crusted bananas wrapped in salmon. A fan of perfect bluefin tuna might be garnished with nods to the local fishing community, which encompasses the Spanish, Cajun French, and Vietnamese. "We are uniquely linked to many cultures here. I try to reflect this in my dishes," said the chef.

The two-time James Beard Award nominee is an alchemist with raw fish. A recent combo included thinly sliced kiwi, curls of sea bream, yuzu vinegar, and white truffle oil, all crowned with pearls of king salmon roe. Perfect fish is adorned with the likes of flower petals, leaves, herbs, bits of fruit, grains of salt, house-made fermented chili oil, and even pickled purple cauliflower juice in a perfect circular pool.

On the hot side of the menu, dishes reflect flavors from the chef's birthplace, like the spicy dan dan noodles, and mala holla, a mound of beef shank sliced paper-thin, spiced with deliciously numbing red and green Sichuan peppercorns. There's a rotating array of dumplings, perhaps a recipe with pork, ginger, and cabbage from his mother's kitchen or tender purses of beef and caramelized onion in curried broth.

Another reason to sit at the chef's counter is to get to know the gregarious chef as he slices, composes, and drizzles. It's clear that every plate Hao creates makes a statement. New Orleans is lucky to have him.

LUVI chef Hao Gong is laser focused on the quality and freshness of fish as being crucial to the success of every dish. The highest-quality Gulf bluefin will be slightly translucent and deep red in color, with a fine, smooth texture. Chef Hao believes his guests eat with their eyes first. As with all of his dishes, this pristine Gulf bluefin is treated and adorned like edible art, with carrots cut to look like flowers, twists of cucumber and lemon, and, at the restaurant, a curl of real gold leaf. For the home cook, microgreens and carrots cut either freehand or with a mold can provide both eye appeal and the necessary mix of flavors and textures. The idea is for flavors and textures to be even throughout the dish, balanced all in one bite.

SERVES 2

TUNA

¾ POUND BLUEFIN TUNA, CUT IN HALF FOR 2 PORTIONS

2 TEASPOONS WILD KING SALMON ROE

4 CUCUMBER TWISTS

2 SLICED CARROT "FLOWERS"

4 LEMON TRIANGLE ZESTS

½ TEASPOON HONEY POWDER OR 1 DROP HONEY PER PIECE OF TUNA

FEW PIECES OF MICROGREENS

SAUCE (PAGE 198)

6 DROPS CALIFORNIA EXTRA-VIRGIN OLIVE OIL

1. Gently place 1 portion bluefin tuna onto cutting board. With sharpened knife, cut tuna into 6 equal pieces.

2. For each portion, put bluefin tuna onto plate of your choosing. Place 1 teaspoon wild king salmon roe on a few bluefin tuna slices.

continued...

3. This step is where you can get creative. Place cucumber twists, carrot flowers, and lemon triangle zests as you wish. Use your eye to place these items where they look the most symmetrical and aesthetically pleasing. Last, strategically place a dash of honey powder or a drop of honey and a few microgreens.

4. Drizzle Sauce on plate, then put 3 drops extra-virgin olive oil as the finish.

SAUCE

¼ CUP CREOLE MUSTARD	2 TABLESPOONS SESAME OIL
1 CUP RICE VINEGAR	½ TABLESPOON YUZU JUICE

1. In bowl, combine all ingredients.

MAMOU

942 North Rampart Street
mamounola.com

A FRENCH NOUVEAU CELEBRATION BETWEEN FRIENDS

Locals might have understandably associated the 2022 opening of MaMou on the edge of the French Quarter with the Evangeline Parish town Mamou, famous for its Cajun music and chicken-chasing Mardi Gras. Instead, the name is connected to the restaurant's chef, Tom Branighan, whose great-grandmother was affectionately known in the family as MaMou.

The restaurant is a collaboration between Tom and longtime friend and master sommelier Molly Wismeier, who came to MaMou after tending the cellars at Restaurant R'evolution. Before that, she worked for Charlie Trotter in Chicago.

Tom, a Louisiana native, learned to love French cuisine while cooking side by side with David Bouley at Café Bouley. David, the chef who introduced nouvelle cuisine to New York City, also brought Daniel Boulud to town and convinced him to open Daniel. David trained under French masters like Joël Robuchon and Paul Bocuse, professionals with many culinary lessons to impart. However, running an inclusive, kind kitchen was not one of them. For Tom, that itself was a lesson.

The partners met when Tom cooked for Molly at the now-shuttered restaurant Balise. He made the pork loin with sauce Robert that is on MaMou's menu today. "I wanted to have my own restaurant, and I saw Tom as the right person to do that with," Molly recalled. Although they started envisioning their restaurant in 2017, between the pandemic and finding the right space, the process took longer than expected. When 942 North Rampart Street became available, the lease was signed in days.

The forty-eight-seat restaurant was redone with art nouveau flourishes. A carpet of blooms stretches across the ceiling against a jewel-tone color scheme. The bar is inspired by Pink Mamma in Paris. A cluster of family photos hangs above a clutch of copper pots, MaMou's photo front and center.

Despite the kitchen's expert execution, there's nothing stuffy about MaMou's compact menu. The salmon mi cuit encases smoked ribbons of fish in a savory beignet, with a waterfall of fresh herbs on top. It's best enjoyed picked up and eaten like a hand pie. Tom's rendition of cassoulet pairs Louisiana red beans and rice with a gratin crust and a few slices of chunky headcheese. The many steps that go into creating a dish like braised celery hearts with smoked beef tongue or poisson à la Florentine with a caviar beurre blanc speak volumes about how passionate Tom is about nouvelle French cuisine.

When he was younger, Tom imagined having a fancy restaurant with a seven-course French tasting menu. Now he's all about an approachable menu that combines tradition with new takes on French dishes. "When you reach thirty, the idea of having a life outside the restaurant is more important than when you were twenty-two. We want that for our staff and for ourselves."

New Orleans-Style Red Bean Cassoulet
See page 204

NEW ORLEANS-STYLE RED BEAN CASSOULET

Chef Tom has reimagined this New Orleans classic through the lens of the traditional French dish from Toulouse. Every time he makes it, he thinks of his father. His dad always kept an eye on him while he was half-heartedly doing his homework at the kitchen table after school. To pass the time, sometimes his dad would cook "Not Ya Momma's Red Beans," a family favorite. At MaMou, house-pickled pork goes into the pot, but store-bought will substitute (they also top it off with a homemade piece of head cheese, which you likely wouldn't make at home but can find in stores). Remember to allow time for the overnight bean soak.

SERVES 6-8

1 POUND DRY RED KIDNEY BEANS

1 POUND PICKLED PORK, SMALL OR MEDIUM DICED

2 LARGE SPANISH ONIONS, MEDIUM DICED

2 LARGE GREEN BELL PEPPERS, SEEDED, MEDIUM DICED

2 LARGE STALKS CELERY, MEDIUM DICED

2 GARLIC CLOVES, PEELED (DO NOT CRUSH TO PEEL)

1 CUP TOMATO PASTE

1 CUP DRY SHERRY

1 CUP DRY WHITE WINE

1 TABLESPOON GARLIC POWDER

1 TABLESPOON ONION POWDER

2 BAY LEAVES

1 TEASPOON SMOKED PAPRIKA

2 QUARTS PORK OR CHICKEN STOCK

SALT AND PEPPER, TO TASTE

1–2 TABLESPOONS PICKLED JALAPEÑO JUICE

1–2 TABLESPOONS CRYSTAL HOT SAUCE

½ CUP UNSALTED BUTTER

DRIED CORNBREAD, AS NEEDED

1. Soak beans in 6-quart container covered in water overnight. Drain the next day.

2. When ready to cook, play "Cry to Me" by Professor Longhair and preheat oven to 350°F.

3. In wide, oven-safe pot, begin searing pickled pork in batches to maintain heat of pan. Once browned, drain pork, reserving fat. Turn heat off until next step, so glaze on bottom of pan does not burn.

4. Add onions to pan and turn heat to medium-low. Caramelize onions, then add rest of trinity and garlic; sweat 10 minutes.

5. Add tomato paste and combine with trinity. Continuously stir over low heat to develop crimson color.

6. Deglaze with sherry and white wine. Cook over low heat until alcohol aroma is gone, about 10 minutes. Stir occasionally.

7. Add beans, garlic powder, onion powder, bay leaves, and paprika; cover with stock, reserving 1 pint as needed at end.

8. Bring to boil and lightly season with salt and pepper. Liquid will reduce and concentrate the flavor, so don't oversalt.

9. Transfer pot to oven and braise, covered, for 1½ hours. The indirect heat will keep beans from burning on bottom.

10. Remove pot from oven. Add pork, stir, season again with salt and pepper to taste, and return to oven for another 1½ hours.

11. After 3 total hours cooking, remove pot and check doneness. Beans should be tender but still have subtle texture while yielding to gentle pressure. Check liquid thickness as well. Add stock as needed. Cook until done. As liquid becomes more viscous, it becomes more difficult for beans to soak in moisture. A little more stock can help. Always add in small quantities. You can always add more, but it's difficult to take out. Keep in mind that you will add jalapeño juice and hot sauce at end for seasoning. Best to keep liquid on the thicker side.

12. Season with jalapeño juice and hot sauce to taste. Stir in butter until fully combined. Here, you are seasoning for acid, not spice. With right amount of acid, there should be a pleasant but not unpalatable amount of heat. The butter is key.

13. Raise oven temperature to 450°F.

14. In food processor, pulse dried cornbread until medium-fine breadcrumbs form.

15. Spoon beans-and-pork mixture into heat-safe bowl or casserole and sprinkle with crumbs until fully covered. Place in oven and bake until golden brown, about 10 minutes. Serve immediately.

MAYPOP

611 O'Keefe Avenue
maypoprestaurant.com

CHEF MICHAEL GULOTTA KEEPS NEW ORLEANS GUESSING

When chef Michael Gulotta opened the cheekily named MoPho in 2014, his mash-up of Southeast Asian and Creole cuisine made big waves. Okay, he's that guy, a wunderkind at fusing flavors and using local ingredients creatively. He got lots of props for his efforts, from a Best New Chef nod from *Food & Wine* to being named one of the Top 30 Chefs to Watch in the nation by *Plate* magazine.

His follow-up restaurant, the less casual Maypop, opened in 2018. And while he continued to mine the foodways of Southeast Asia, powered by local flavors including tasso, crawfish, and Gulf-caught sheepshead, he stretched a bit further, introducing house-made pastas and Italian charcuterie like culatello, a slightly leaner cousin to prosciutto.

Again, the accolades. From a New Orleans top-twenty restaurant by *Condé Nast Traveler* to being named one of the twenty-two Most Essential Food and Drink Experiences in New Orleans by Thrillist, Michael clearly was onto something. In 2019, his team opened a second MoPho location in the new Louis Armstrong New Orleans International Airport. He was a finalist for the James Beard Award for Best Chef: South in 2020.

When the pandemic changed the restaurant world, likely forever, MoPho hung on. Michael shut Maypop down for thirteen months. When it reopened, the chef's Italian roots were more apparent, though nouc cham, Vietnamese fish sauce, was still in rotation. If anything, his interplay between cultures was expanded and refined.

In 2023, he opened Tana, a concept that had a three-year run as a bar pop-up back in 2016. Conceived as an ambitious Italian kitchen inside the now-closed Mid-City bar Trèo, Tana served Sicilian-style plates like garlic spaghetti with clams and sausage and grilled snapper with harissa-roasted cauliflower. While the new project may seem like a major shift in focus for the chef, fans of his cooking recognize a return to his culinary roots.

Michael, like so many New Orleans natives, has Sicilian blood. Most of the Italians who immigrated to the city in the late 1800s came from Sicily. They opened groceries and fruit stands, many settling in the lower end of the French Quarter, which earned the neighborhood the nickname Little Palermo.

Those family roots loom large for Michael, who named the new restaurant for his great-grandmother. Notable Sicilian dishes are influenced by Gaetana—nicknamed Tana. Tana is a spacious upscale restaurant in the monied Jefferson Parish town of Old Metairie. There is an emphasis on fresh pasta dishes, including a prominent pasta rolling station that lets diners see the chef in action.

Michael is only in his forties, so what's next is anybody's guess. The chef clearly gives himself license to indulge his imagination, which, for the many fans of his cuisine, is a good thing indeed.

WILD LOUISIANA CRAWFISH TOM YUM WITH GNOCCHETTI PASTA

Of course chef Michael dreams up a version of the spicy Thai soup tom yum that incorporates Louisiana crawfish. Michael is a culinary whiz with a penchant for blending the flavors of the Mekong Delta with ingredients from the Mississippi Delta, first at his restaurant MoPho, opened in 2014, and here, from the menu of Maypop, which opened in 2018. His Sicilian heritage emerges with handmade pastas, a penchant he takes to the next level at his latest restaurant, Tana, opened in 2023. The fermented crab paste, found in jars or tubes at most Asian grocers, brings a critical nuanced funk to this boldly flavored version of the Thai specialty.

SERVES 4

½ POUND DRIED GNOCCHETTI PASTA, COOKED AL DENTE, WITH SOME LIQUID RESERVED

1 BATCH TOM YUM BUTTER (PAGE 210)

½ POUND PICKED CRAWFISH TAILS

2 TABLESPOONS PICKLED MIRLITON OR EGGPLANT

½ CUP CITRUS HERB CRUST, FOR SPRINKLING (PAGE 211)

1 TABLESPOON SLICED CHIVES, FOR SPRINKLING

2 TABLESPOONS GRATED GRANA PADANO OR PARMIGIANO-REGGIANO CHEESE, FOR SPRINKLING

1. Simmer cooked gnocchetti in Tom Yum Butter 2 minutes.

2. Gently fold in crawfish tails and pickled mirliton or eggplant and heat just to warm through.

3. Divide pasta among 4 bowls and top each with healthy sprinkle Citrus Herb Crust, chives, and grated Grana Padano or Parmigiano-Reggiano cheese.

continued...

TOM YUM BUTTER

SERVES 4

1 TABLESPOON VIRGIN
COCONUT OIL

2 SHALLOTS, MINCED

1 RED BELL PEPPER, SEEDED
AND SMALL DICED

1 THAI CHILE

3 GARLIC CLOVES, SLICED

2 TABLESPOONS MINCED GINGER

1 STALK LEMONGRASS, SLICED
THINLY INTO RINGS

1 LIME LEAF

1 TEASPOON FERMENTED
CRAB PASTE

1 CUP SHELLFISH OR CHICKEN STOCK

⅓ CUP COCONUT MILK

½ CUP UNSALTED BUTTER

2 TABLESPOONS RENDERED
BACON FAT

½ BUNCH CILANTRO,
FINELY CHOPPED

JUICE AND ZEST OF 2 LIMES

FISH SAUCE, TO TASTE

1. In nonreactive pan, warm coconut oil over medium-high heat.

2. Add shallots, red pepper, Thai chile, garlic, ginger, and lemongrass and sweat 3 minutes. Do not caramelize.

3. Add lime leaf and crab paste and sweat an additional 2 minutes.

4. Pour in stock and coconut milk and bring to simmer.

5. Whisk in butter and bacon fat to emulsify.

6. Finish with cilantro, lime juice and zest, and fish sauce, cut heat, and let steep.

7. Check seasoning and adjust to taste.

CITRUS HERB CRUST

SERVES 4

½ CUP NEUTRAL OIL

1 GARLIC CLOVE

½ BUNCH CILANTRO

JUICE AND ZEST OF 1 ORANGE

¼ CUP GRATED GRANA PADANO OR PARMIGIANO-REGGIANO CHEESE

1 CUP PANKO BREADCRUMBS, LIGHTLY TOASTED

1. In blender, puree oil, garlic, cilantro, orange juice and zest, and Grana Padano or Parmigiano-Reggiano to a fine paste.

2. In medium bowl, fold together herb puree and toasted panko and spread on baking sheet to dry.

MISTER MAO

4501 Tchoupitoulas Street
mistermaonola.com

CHEF SOPHINA WELCOMES THE ADVENTUROUS

Mister Mao is a restaurant that should come with a safe word.

Irreverently conceived by chef Sophina Uong and her husband/partner, William "Wildcat" Greenwell, Mister Mao is a dizzying sum of its Technicolor parts. Channeling bold Asian and Mexican flavors, the chef isn't one bit interested in the F-word—fusion is not her jam. Instead, she mood boards fiercely creative dishes that speak to what she loves to eat. This is a woman who cooks like she's got nothing to lose.

Early guests may have stumbled into the corner Creole cottage on Tchoupitoulas Uptown, thinking Mister Mao was a Chinese restaurant. Nope, the restaurant was named for the chef's dearly departed cat. Polyglot flavors are second nature to this fearless chef. The couple lived in the Bay Area for years, addicted to visiting restaurants inspired by other cultures. They love Thai flavors, hot spice, and riffs on Southern cuisine using locally sourced ingredients. Proudly "inauthentic," Mister Mao doesn't pretend to appeal to the masses.

The restaurant's vibe is drop-dead sexy, with a Tarzan-meets–Maurice Sendak décor that includes an arresting tiger mural from NOLA artist Margie Tillman Ayres. The bar, Naked Bill's, is William's purview, with drolly named cocktails (some tiki-inspired), an eclectic wine list, and a robust lineup of no- and low-alcohol libations.

Sophina is self-taught. She worked her way from the front of the house to the kitchen, where she clearly belongs. Her CV includes Bay Area restaurants Waterbar, Revival Bar + Kitchen, Calavera, and Absinthe Brasserie & Bar. After she was named Food Network's *Chopped Grill Masters* Grand Champion in Napa. She was hired to manage Andrew Zimmern's Lucky Cricket restaurant in Minneapolis. When that project tanked, the couple decided to move to either Manhattan or New Orleans. Opting for NOLA, they leased the former Dick & Jenny's space just a few weeks prior to the citywide pandemic shutdown, finally opening in the summer of 2021.

Although her heritage is Cambodian, Sophina didn't grow up with that cuisine. She was born there and fled the war-torn country for America with her family when she was a tot. She grew up in Long Beach, but Cambodian dishes weren't what was for dinner. "I cooked for my dad and brother out of *Betty Crocker's Microwave Cookbook*," she recalled. She grew up in a multicultural neighborhood and spent hours watching mothers and grandmothers cook everything from traditional American fare to homemade tortillas. Her palate expanded in all directions.

Sophina produces her dishes with precision. Take the stellar starter, pani puri. Crispy lentil cups are filled with potato masala, seasonal fruit, and chutney. The server pours a deeply green spicy mint broth into each cup. Devour in one bite for a synchronized explosion of textures and flavors. The Kashmiri fried chicken is another menu anchor, a pulsating hot bird spiced Pakistani style. This is a convivial restaurant, lively and unapologetic, which suits chef Sophina just fine. "We welcome all, but we also know we aren't for everyone."

MISTER MAO GINGER SALAD

This salad isn't for the faint of heart. At Mister Mao, chef Sophina is known for her startlingly original Asian roadhouse cuisine with a backbeat of tiki sensibility—fierce flavors that are the opposite of demure. This ginger salad is a case in point: a bright, crunchy treat with a surprise in every bite, and a toss that needs time for chopping, deep-frying, and stirring. Adding the toasted dark chickpea flour brings nuttiness and depth to the salad while keeping it gluten-free. If you're short on time, two bags of store-made coleslaw mix can substitute for the veggies.

SERVES 6-8

CRUNCHY BITS

½ CUP RAW SUNFLOWER SEEDS

1 CUP PEANUTS

3 TABLESPOONS NEUTRAL OIL

1 TABLESPOON KOSHER SALT, PLUS MORE TO TASTE

1 CUP CANNED CHICKPEAS

1. Preheat oven to 300°F. Spread sunflower seeds and peanuts evenly on baking pan. Drizzle with 1 tablespoon oil and season with 1½ teaspoons salt. Roast 30–40 minutes or until golden brown, stirring occasionally.

2. Dry chickpeas with paper towels. They must be dry to get crispy. Heat 2 tablespoons oil in skillet over medium-high heat. Add chickpeas. Cook 8–10 minutes until very dry and golden, and crisp on outside. Season with remaining salt, plus more as needed to taste.

continued...

FUN THINGS

2 TABLESPOONS CURRANTS

¼ CUP SHERRY VINEGAR

1 TABLESPOON CHICKPEA FLOUR

1 CUP TAMARIND DATE CHUTNEY

1. In small bowl, cover currants in sherry vinegar and let sit 15 minutes. Drain and set aside.

2. Heat nonstick skillet over medium heat. Add chickpea flour and stir until toasty and dark brown in color, about 5 minutes. Set aside.

VEGGIES

8 CUPS SHAVED CABBAGE

2 CUPS LUNCHBOX
SWEET PEPPERS, SHAVED

2 CUPS SHAVED RED ONION

2 CUPS SHREDDED CARROTS

2 CUPS CILANTRO, CHOPPED,
PLUS MORE TO TASTE

2 TABLESPOONS
JULIENNED GINGER

3 SERRANO CHILES, SLICED THIN

KOSHER SALT, TO TASTE

1. Mix all ingredients in bowl.

To Serve

1. Toss Crunchy Bits, Fun Things, and Veggies together in bowl. Add salt to taste; result should be spicy, sweet, crunchy, and earthy, all in one bite.

MUCHO MÁS

8201 Oak Street

WHAT HAPPENS WHEN A CHEF STARTS OVER

It's not unusual for a chef to start out in the business washing dishes, but when Julio Machado came to New Orleans, the culinary school graduate had run a food consulting business in his home country of Venezuela for a decade, providing companies in South America and Europe with product development. "I was successful in my work. I worked hard."

Then everything changed.

In February 2018, his business and worldly assets were stolen from him by forces aligned with the Venezuelan government.

It was like something out of a movie. There was a knock on his door, and he was given two choices. "They said, 'We take everything from you, and you leave right now. We will take you to the airport. Or we will take you to jail.' I know that meant I'd never be heard from again." He was in Miami six hours later. "They took my belt, my shoes, the titles to my cars—everything—except they didn't find one small bank account."

So, with $3,000 to his name, the chef started over. He was granted political asylum and permanent residency in a matter of months, moving to New Orleans to be close to family.

Despite his experience and expertise, the only restaurant job he could get was washing dishes at Lakeview Harbor, a casual burger joint by the lake. "My English wasn't so good," said Julio. Owner Shawn Toups took notice of his dishwasher's talents, befriended him, and added prep to his job description.

He moved on to cooking at a steak house and then a Mexican restaurant in Metairie, his first experience with Mexican food. "It's much different from Venezuelan cuisine." He was a partner in a place called Tacos del Cartel, also in Metairie, then went in a different direction.

He approached Toups about opening a place together, which they did in January 2023, five years since the chef was forced to leave his home country. The name, which means "much more," was inspired by his customers' requests for a bigger menu at the compact Tacos del Cartel. "They were always asking me for more. Now I can give it to them."

The ninety-five-seat restaurant is patterned after the hip scene in Mexico City, with Asian influences figuring into the mix. There is a modern bar, blue-velvet seating, and neon lighting for a groovy lounge effect.

The menu brings deeply flavorful dishes to the table. Guacamole, empanadas, quesadillas, and queso fundido, accented with house-made pork cracklins, are a few of the starters. Steak ceviche is cured with rice wine vinegar, citrus, chili, cilantro, and garlic and served sliced, with corn tortillas.

Mexican ramen introduces soy, ginger, and garlic to either pork loin or chicken breast, with rice noodles swimming in a flavorful broth. Birria tacos are filled with smoky barbecued brisket. Potent cocktails, including supersized batches to share, punctuate the menu. "I love New Orleans. This is my dream," said Julio. "It's another chapter."

Chef Julio has now moved on to his own place, Como Arepas, Uptown. In addition to Como Arepas, Julio opened Origin—a Venzuelan restaurant that pays homage to his personal culinary roots in Bywater—in early spring 2024.

ROASTED CHICKEN QUESO TACOS

Chicken tacos are an easy choice for a weeknight family dinner or for feeding a game-day crowd. The dish is perfect for using up leftover roast chicken, or even a grocery store rotisserie chicken to really save time. This simple recipe adds the gooey goodness of melted cheese and crisped corn tortillas for extra flavor and texture. Chef Julio reminds us that tacos are a fun, social food that easily turns into a party. Why not set up a fixings bar, with a range of options like pickled jalapeños, cilantro, sour cream, and peppers in adobo, and let everybody make their own? And don't forget the hot sauce.

SERVES 4

3 CUPS SHREDDED ROAST CHICKEN

8 CORN TORTILLAS

1½ CUPS GRATED MONTEREY JACK OR ANY CHEESE OF YOUR CHOICE

1 CUP SHREDDED LETTUCE, FOR TOPPING

½ RED ONION, SLICED, FOR TOPPING

CILANTRO, FOR TOPPING

1 RIPE AVOCADO, SLICED, FOR TOPPING

KOSHER SALT, TO TASTE

SALSA, FOR SERVING

1. Heat chicken in nonstick pan and set aside.

2. Over medium heat, spray a little oil in pan and add a tortilla. Warm 1 minute and then flip.

3. Add an eighth of the cheese and chicken. Use spatula to fold tortilla into taco shape and cook, pressing down with spatula occasionally until tortilla is crispy and cheese is melted. Make sure to cook tortilla on both sides to get a crunchy texture. Repeat steps 2 and 3 with remaining tortillas.

4. Serve on plate topped with lettuce, onion, cilantro, avocado, and pinch of salt. Serve with your favorite salsa.

QUEEN TRINI LISA

4200 D'Hemecourt Street
queentrinilisa.com

BRINGING ISLAND SOUL CUISINE TO NEW ORLEANS

For the uninitiated, Trinidadian food has a strong personality and sense of place. While there is certainly overlap in foods found in neighboring islands, the sister islands of Trinidad and Tobago dish bold flavors influenced by African, East Indian, and Asian cultures.

When Lisa "Queen Trini" Nelson started making food for her kids when they'd come to her Bywater corner store to do their homework after school, her customers wanted in. Although her menu carried the usual New Orleans favorites like fried chicken and hot sausage po'boys, it was the chicken curry, rice and peas, and coco bread fish sandwich that they craved.

Lisa has come a long way from the village of Hardbargain, where she was raised in Trinidad. She put down roots in New Orleans when her family came to help rebuild the city after Katrina, raising her four children in the city she now calls home. After closing the corner store, she started popping up with her Caribbean soul food in bars around town. The self-trained chef opened her own restaurant, Queen Trini Lisa Island Soul Food, in Mid-City at the end of 2021.

The restaurant is a cozy spot, with red benches outside and seating for twenty in the bright and airy dining room decorated with an original mural of island scenes and flags from her home country. Her love of cooking tracks back to when she was young, helping her mom prepare food for the family.

Lisa brings New Orleans flavors into her dishes, like using Creole seasoning in her doubles, the vegan street food that starts with puffy flatbread laced with turmeric, folded (or "doubled") over curried chickpeas bright with notes of coriander and tamarind. She taught herself how to make the spongy turmeric flatbread. "I couldn't get anybody to share the real recipe, so I kept working on it until it tasted right."

Then there's her chicken curry, warmed with spices with just a touch of heat on the back end, served with rice and peas, Caribbean-style spinach, and fried plantains on the side. Coco bread is a Jamaican staple, with a firm crust and a soft, slightly sweet crumb. For her coco bread fish sandwich, Lisa splits the bread open and fills it with catfish crusted in Louisiana-style fish fry, sliced pineapple, sweet fried plantains, cucumber, and tomato.

Lisa finds a welcome synergy in cooking Trinidadian food for folks living in the Big Easy. "There's a lot here that reminds me of home."

Soft-spoken and warm, Lisa is anything but a princess type, but Queen Trini is a name that's stuck. The nickname started as something catchy for social media. "Now it's what people call me. It's easy to remember."

QUEEN TRINI'S CURRIED CHICKEN

In chef Queen Trini's kitchen, the flavors of her native Trinidad inform everything from barbecue jerk chicken to doubles, a vegan Trinidadian street food made of curried chickpeas sandwiched inside a turmeric-laced flatbread. Her curry chicken is a crowd-pleaser, marinated overnight and steeped with flavor. In a pinch, an hour in the fridge will do. The longer the chicken marinates, the deeper the curry flavor.

SERVES 6

4 POUNDS CHICKEN LEGS AND THIGHS, RINSED, SKIN AND FAT REMOVED

2 TEASPOONS KOSHER SALT

1 MEDIUM ONION, HALVED

8 GARLIC CLOVES

8 SPRIGS CILANTRO

CRACKED BLACK PEPPER, TO TASTE

1 JALAPEÑO PEPPER, SEEDED AND SLICED (OPTIONAL)

2 TABLESPOONS CURRY POWDER

2 TEASPOONS TURMERIC

1⅔–2⅔ CUPS WATER, PLUS MORE AS NEEDED

¼ CUP VEGETABLE OIL

2 POTATOES, BOILED, ROUGH CHOPPED (OPTIONAL)

SALT AND PEPPER, TO TASTE

COOKED RICE, FOR SERVING

1. Place chicken in bowl. Sprinkle with salt.

2. In food processor, chop half onion with garlic, cilantro, black pepper, and jalapeño, if using.

3. Add mixture to bowl. Stir mixture together so chicken is totally coated in seasoning ingredients. Marinate chicken at least 2 hours in refrigerator.

4. When ready to cook, make curry slurry: add curry powder and turmeric to bowl. Pour in ⅔ cup water and stir until dissolved.

5. In large skillet, heat vegetable oil over medium-low heat. Pour in curry slurry and cook a few minutes, stirring constantly. Curry slurry will deepen in color. If mixture becomes too dry during cooking, add a little water.

6. When curry slurry has become a thick paste, chop other half onion and add to slurry, allowing onion to soften, about 5 minutes.

7. Add chicken. Stir to coat, then cook, pan half-covered, 5 minutes. Turn chicken, then add 1 to 2 cups water. Shake pan and allow chicken to cook until done, stirring every 5 minutes. Add potatoes, if using. Cook about 20 minutes.

8. Season with salt and pepper to taste. Serve chicken over rice, with plenty of curry slurry on top.

ROSEDALE

801 Rosedale Drive
rosedalerestaurant.com

SUSAN SPICER STILL DOING WHAT SHE LOVES

On a list of chefs who have shaped the New Orleans culinary scene, Susan Spicer's name would be right at the top. Susan has spent more than four decades on her craft, creating modern globally influenced American cuisine before everybody else was thinking outside the box.

In a city known for its flash and glitter, Susan is an understated star. She's soft-spoken and has described herself as shy. Yet her influence, the number of chefs she's mentored, and her insistence on a kind kitchen before it was a thing all speak to what sort of woman she is and how she leads.

Now in her early seventies, Susan is thinking about what comes next. She is still doing what she loves, cooking on the line at Rosedale, a sweet neighborhood restaurant in Mid-

City. The chef's talked about teaching, writing another book. Her longtime customers wish fervently for her to keep cooking for them.

At the glittering Four Seasons Hotel New Orleans 2023 gala where she was awarded the Ella Brennan Lifetime Achievement in Hospitality Award, presented by the New Orleans Wine & Food Experience, her praises were sung by chef after chef. Finally, her husband, Chip Martinson, took the dais and told the crowd he wants to spend more time with his wife. Some pandemic habits are hard to break.

At twenty-six, she started her career under chef Daniel Bonnot at the Louis XVI Restaurant. Susan opened a bistro inside the Hotel Maison de Ville in 1985, and, with business partner Regina Keever, opened Bayona in 1990. She won a James Beard Award in 1993.

Along the way, she's seen great changes, both in the New Orleans and the American culinary scene. She names the accessibility of global products as one of the single biggest game changers.

In the 1990s, Susan pioneered the use of international ingredients that challenged the long-held definition of New Orleans cuisine. At Bayona, she spun the globe, bringing influences from Spain, Italy, and France into play, along with flavors of the Mediterranean, India, and Asia. Now, her focus is on her Rosedale venue, where a daily changing menu spotlights local and seasonal ingredients. Preserved lemons show up in a Caesar salad, Alsatian choucroute pairs with salmon, Mississippi rabbit is stuffed with sausage and served with smothered greens and dirty rice. Her kitchen is as forward-thinking as it was four decades ago.

At Rosedale, the menu of Southern-inspired comfort food is anything but predictable. The meatloaf sandwich is smeared with roasted garlic aioli and bacon jam, with a tangle of arugula peeking out of the ciabatta roll. There is traditional buttery Worcestershire shrimp, and a lemony taramasalata, Greek fish roe spread served with pita chips. Fried chicken arrives glossy with Tabasco honey. Nothing trendy to see here. This is uncluttered cooking that depends on the brilliance of its ingredients to shine.

For more than forty years, Susan has helped shape the local dining scene, pioneering new possibilities in the New Orleans kitchen. And through it all, she's cooked, which she continues to do at Rosedale today.

ITALIAN-STYLE BROCCOLI

Chef Susan may be globally acclaimed, the founder of several successful restaurants, and the winner of multiple awards, but she's anything but fancy. Down-to-earth, warm, and ever passionate about making great food, she spends most of her time at Rosedale, a casual neighborhood eatery tucked away in Mid-City. Located in the building that housed the Third District police station for half a century, Rosedale serves straightforward food steeped in New Orleans tradition, without a bit of pretense on the plate. This recipe illustrates Susan's style perfectly, with the emphasis on fresh ingredients and simple presentation.

SERVES 4

1 LARGE HEAD BROCCOLI, STEM TRIMMED, CUT INTO 3-INCH PIECES—ABOUT 6 CUPS

¼ CUP OLIVE OIL

1 TABLESPOON MINCED ROSEMARY

1 TEASPOON KOSHER SALT, PLUS MORE AS NEEDED

½ TEASPOON MINCED GARLIC, PLUS MORE AS NEEDED

¼ TEASPOON RED PEPPER FLAKES, PLUS MORE AS NEEDED

6 TABLESPOONS GRATED PARMESAN OR PECORINO CHEESE, FOR TOPPING

1. Bring 1 gallon salted water to boil in pot with lid. When water is at full boil, add broccoli and submerge.

2. Cook 1–2 minutes, then drain and add broccoli to large bowl ice water to shock.

3. Let chill and drain. This can be done several hours or even the day before serving.

4. In large sauté pan, heat half the olive oil until shimmering and add broccoli.

5. Toss or stir to coat with olive oil, then sprinkle in rosemary, salt, garlic, and red pepper flakes and stir again. Turn burner to medium-high heat and let broccoli cook undisturbed 3–4 minutes, then carefully add 1–2 tablespoons water to create steam. This will heat the broccoli evenly.

6. Toss or stir again and add rest of olive oil. Cook broccoli until it starts to color a bit and maybe get some crisp bits. Taste for seasoning and add more of whatever you think it needs. Some people like it hotter or more garlicky.

7. Toss again, then remove broccoli to platter or individual plates and top with grated cheese. Serve immediately.

SABA

5757 Magazine Street
eatwithsaba.com

ALON SHAYA FINDS HIMSELF TIED TO HIS ISRAELI ROOTS

Alon Shaya's personal journey to become a chef and start a business, Pomegranate Hospitality, with his wife and partner, Emily, is well-documented. The couple has opened three restaurants since 2018: Saba, which means grandfather in Hebrew, in Uptown in New Orleans; Safta, which means grandmother in Hebrew, in Denver; and Miss River, an upscale ode to the New Orleans tradition of grand dining, in the Four Seasons Hotel New Orleans. He also oversees small plates at the hotel's stunning Chandelier Bar.

When you meet the Israeli-born chef, who came to the United States at the age of four, he seems the definition of a mensch, a nice guy who tries to do the right thing. But his journey into the kitchen wasn't an easy one. A problem kid, he was always in trouble. Donna Barnett, Alon's former home economics teacher at his suburban Philadelphia high school, is the mentor who helped the wayward teen find a purpose in life. Because of her, he went to the Culinary Institute of America. He found his passion.

The two now have the Shaya Barnett Foundation together, dedicated to providing a culinary or hospitality track for high school juniors and seniors in underserved areas of New Orleans.

In his memoir, *Shaya: An Odyssey of Food, My Journey Back to Israel,* Alon reflects on the personal and professional journey that empowered him to connect with his heritage through food. With influences that stem from the Middle East, Europe, and North Africa, the restaurant Saba represents a collection of moments where food and culture cross paths.

Alon spent time in Italy before opening Domenica with chef John Besh in the Roosevelt Hotel, a regional Italian restaurant with homemade pasta and an impressive wine cellar. In 2015, Alon won the James Beard Award for Best Chef: South for his cooking there. He next was a partner in the restaurant Shaya, his first deep dive into Israeli cuisine. He is no longer associated with that restaurant, finding his way home with the opening of Saba.

Alon's food pops with color and flavor. Tender harissa-roasted chicken is coated with a burnt sienna–tinged paste, simply presented with wedges of lemon. There's bright-green falafel served with tahini and zhoug. Foie gras pairs with toasted challah and a drizzle of rose tahini. Chicken schnitzel is served with shaved cabbage, labneh, and dill. This is food that brings joy.

The Pomegranate Hospitality mission statement reflects exactly how Alon and Emily run their businesses. It speaks volumes about what matters to them both.

> We will spend our days together in a place where everyone feels comfortable and safe. We will create a space, whether in our restaurant or throughout our community and beyond focused on furthering love, mutual respect and professional and personal fulfillment. We will stand up for and uphold our values of equality for all people no matter the circumstances. We will surround ourselves with people who share in these values. Then, we will cook and serve, and be happy.

ROASTED SPECKLED TROUT WITH TAHINI AND PINE NUTS

Chef Alon recalls cooking a version of this dish with his sister in North Carolina, where he'd evacuated after Hurricane Katrina. Post-Katrina, the homey flavors were just the thing he wanted and needed to eat. This takes no time at all to prepare and is a fantastic example of the marriage of seafood and tahini, which may be completely unexpected for the uninitiated; it's an Israeli version of the classic New Orleans pairing of fish and brown butter. Any delicate white fish will work beautifully.

SERVES 2-4

1 TABLESPOON FRESH LEMON JUICE

½ GARLIC CLOVE, CRUSHED

¼ CUP TAHINI

1¼ TEASPOONS KOSHER SALT

3 TABLESPOONS ICE WATER, PLUS MORE AS NEEDED

¼ CUP EXTRA-VIRGIN OLIVE OIL

1½–2 POUNDS SKINLESS TROUT FILLETS

2 TEASPOONS SESAME SEEDS

1 TEASPOON CORIANDER

¼ CUP SEAFOOD, CHICKEN, OR VEGETABLE STOCK

¼ CUP PINE NUTS, TOASTED, FOR TOPPING

5 OR 6 MINT LEAVES, CHOPPED, FOR TOPPING

1 TABLESPOON LIGHTLY PACKED CILANTRO LEAVES, CHOPPED, FOR TOPPING

1 TABLESPOON LIGHTLY PACKED PARSLEY LEAVES, CHOPPED, FOR TOPPING

1. Preheat oven to 400°F.

2. Combine lemon juice and garlic in nonreactive bowl and steep at least 20 minutes, until juice is thoroughly infused.

continued...

3. Strain lemon juice, add to tahini with ¼ teaspoon salt, and beat with electric mixer on medium speed. Mixture will seize up at first, but then it will be incorporated.

4. Once mixture has uniformly fudgy consistency, slowly add ice water and beat on high. Again, it may seize up or look curdled but should smooth out into a thick mousse. If it doesn't, add more water, ½ tablespoon at a time. Set aside.

5. Spread 2 tablespoons olive oil over rimmed baking sheet. Arrange trout fillets side by side on sheet and drizzle remaining olive oil over them, along with sesame seeds, coriander, and remaining 1 teaspoon salt.

6. Roast fish 8–10 minutes or until it is opaque and easily yields to fork. Gently transfer fillets to serving plate.

7. While fish bakes, combine tahini mixture and stock in small saucepan and whisk over low heat until sauce is just warm. To serve, pour sauce over fish, then top with pine nuts and herbs.

SAINT JOHN

1117 Decatur Street
saintjohnnola.com

REVIVING OLD-SCHOOL CREOLE GOODNESS IN THE FRENCH QUARTER

Growing up in a family of New Orleans cooks, Daren Porretto mastered Cajun and Creole Louisiana staples at a young age in his grandparents' kitchen.

Today he oversees the dynamic kitchen at Saint John, the modern and art-filled restaurant in the lower residential end of the French Quarter. Chef/owner Eric Cook opened the restaurant in October 2021. Saint John's foundational menu is rooted in eighteenth-century Creole cookery, with complex dishes that might have crowded a lavish Sunday dinner table back in the day.

Recipes were culled from vintage cookbooks and family traditions in crafting a menu reflective of the cultural influences—Sicilian, French, Spanish, African, German, and Caribbean—that came together over centuries to underpin New Orleans's celebrated cuisine.

The range of vintage cookbooks wherein these recipes were found included *River Road Recipes*, from 1959; *The Jemima Code*, which mines more than 150 Black cookbooks dating back to 1827—a collection that showcases the huge impact Black women chefs have had on the American table; and *La Bonne Cuisine*, first published in 1981 by the women of All Saints' Episcopal Church in River Ridge.

"I've been trying to get *La Bonne Cuisine* from my grandmother for years," said Daren. "She finally gave it to me—with all its little notes and spotted recipes." The retro Creole dishes on Saint John's menu open a world of flavor, resonating with nostalgia for New Orleanians who have celebrated family milestones over platters of chicken Clemenceau and oyster patties. Dishes like chicken and shrimp maque choux, court bouillon, and pork-belly cassoulet all reveal the diversity of influences that created New Orleans cuisine.

The changing menu might include chargrilled filet with crispy oysters and oyster dressing, and turkey necks smothered in rich brown gravy and caramelized onions, with potato salad on the side. There's brown butter–seared scallops with grits, deviled crab with Creole ravigote, and Creole beef daube. Crawfish étouffée swims with buttery Breaux Bridge crawfish tails in a sauce built on a brown roux served over steamed Louisiana popcorn rice.

Diners can get in on the action if they can nab one of twelve coveted seats at the marble chefs' counter looking into an open kitchen.

The restaurant's vibrancy carries over into the décor, with a colorful mural showcasing some of the city's deceased culinary heroes, including Paul Prudhomme. The second-floor dining room features balcony seating over Decatur Street.

Eric, a New Orleans native, brought elevated Southern cuisine to the plate at Gris-Gris, which he opened in the Lower Garden District in 2018. "I didn't grow up eating blackened redfish and chargrilled oysters," he said. "I wanted to get back to real Southern roots, to elevate the kind of home cooking so many of us grew up with."

MACARONI PIE WITH CREOLE RED GRAVY

This ultrarich macaroni pie is a dish that's been close to chef Daren's heart for years. He grew up making macaroni pie with his family. Every time he prepares the meal, it brings back the nostalgia of simpler times at family holiday gatherings. He calls it the ultimate comfort dish—a big hug from his granny in every bite. Unlike traditional marinara sauce, Creole Red Gravy is made with canned Italian crushed tomatoes rather than fresh tomatoes. It will keep, frozen, for up to two months, an easy grab as a base for any dish in need of tomato sauce.

SERVES 8

1 TABLESPOON KOSHER SALT

2 (12-OUNCE) BOXES DRIED BUCATINI PASTA

UNSALTED BUTTER, AS NEEDED, FOR GREASING BAKING DISH

10 CUPS (2½ QUARTS) HEAVY CREAM

4 EGGS

5 CUPS SHREDDED CHEDDAR CHEESE

½ TEASPOON WHITE PEPPER

CREOLE RED GRAVY (PAGE 240)

1. Preheat oven to 375°F.

2. Add salt to large pot of water and bring to boil over high heat. Cook bucatini until al dente, about 7 minutes. Drain but do not rinse.

3. Generously butter glass 9 x 13–inch casserole dish.

4. Add cooked bucatini to baking dish.

5. Add heavy cream to substantial pot, preferably cast-iron Dutch oven, over medium-low heat.

6. While cream is heating, whisk eggs in medium bowl.

7. When cream is just warm to touch, temper eggs by adding large ladle of warm cream to them while whisking constantly.

8. Add tempered eggs to cream in pot and whisk to combine. Add 4 cups shredded cheddar cheese and white pepper to custard, increase heat to medium, and whisk until cheese has melted.

9. Ladle cheese custard over cooked bucatini in baking dish. Use spatula to ensure custard is coating pasta thoroughly, moving coated pasta into corners of dish and smoothing top.

10. Sprinkle remaining 1 cup cheese evenly over top of casserole and bake, uncovered, until golden, bubbly, and thick, about 30 minutes.

11. Allow casserole to cool and set, 15–20 minutes.

12. Cut casserole into 8 even squares and carefully remove each from baking dish with thin spatula. Serve each portion atop small pool Creole Red Gravy.

continued...

CREOLE RED GRAVY

YIELDS 2½ QUARTS

2 TABLESPOONS BLENDED 80% CANOLA/20% OLIVE OIL

2 TEASPOONS RED PEPPER FLAKES

1 CUP FINELY DICED ONION

½ CUP FINELY DICED CELERY

½ CUP FINELY DICED CARROT

3 TABLESPOONS TOMATO PASTE

1 TEASPOON CHOPPED GARLIC

1 (36-OUNCE) CAN DICED TOMATOES, UNDRAINED

1 CUP WATER

½ CUP QUALITY BEEF STOCK

1 BAY LEAF

KOSHER SALT, TO TASTE

1. Heat oil in large pot, preferably cast-iron Dutch oven, over medium heat.

2. Add red pepper flakes and cook, stirring constantly, until oil is infused with flavor. Oil will be color of saffron.

3. Add onion, celery, and carrot and cook, stirring frequently, until vegetables have softened, 5–7 minutes.

4. Add tomato paste and stir to thoroughly coat vegetables.

5. Continue cooking, undisturbed, until deep, brick-colored fond develops on bottom of pot, about 8 minutes.

6. Add garlic, stir to combine, and cook until fragrant, about 1 minute.

7. Add diced tomatoes, water, beef stock, and bay leaf. Use wooden spoon to scrape fond from bottom of pot and blend into sauce.

8. Bring sauce to simmer and cook, stirring occasionally, until it has thickened and vegetables have broken down, about 25 minutes.

9. Carefully remove pot from stove. Remove bay leaf and, using immersion blender, process sauce until nearly smooth. Season to taste with salt.

SAN LORENZO

1507 Magazine Street
saintvincentnola.com

**CREATIVE COASTAL ITALIAN RESTAURANT ANCHORS
THE STYLISH HOTEL SAINT VINCENT**

Dining at San Lorenzo in the Hotel Saint Vincent feels like an Italian holiday, and that's no accident. Its menu of coastal cuisine was inspired by Le Sirenuse in Positano, along the Amalfi Coast. And its handsome white-tablecloth design, with carved columns and wood paneling, channels Da Giacomo in Milan, one of the owners' favorite restaurants.

Despite facing the rigors of the pandemic and Hurricane Ida, the Hotel Saint Vincent opened its doors in 2022, transforming an imposing former orphanage into a gorgeous seventy-five-room boutique hotel oozing high style.

The red-brick building that houses the hotel was built in 1861 as the Saint Vincent's Infant Asylum by Irish immigrant Margaret Haughery, a bakery owner and philanthropist. The building fell into disrepair until local developers partnered with Austin-based MML Hospitality for the $22.2 million redo.

Chef Laura Collins oversees the dining at the Hotel Saint Vincent, which includes San Lorenzo, the Vietnamese-accented Elizabeth Street Café, and whatever private dining is going on in the swank enclave, which has event space for up to three hundred people.

Laura is self-taught and fearless in the kitchen. She was drizzling olive oil over avocados when she was five. The chef worked her way up in kitchens and catering gigs before cooking for five years in Vegas, where she honed her fine dining chops in Wolfgang Puck restaurants. During the pandemic, she worked at a glamping resort near Austin, then was a private chef for a Malibu developer and his family at their Kauai beach house for a year. When she circled back to Austin, she was hired by MML to work at one of their downtown bakeries. As the hotel's opening neared, with Mardi Gras crowds looming and staffing shortages ongoing, she volunteered to come to New Orleans to lead the kitchen team. Her mom is from here, and she spent some time in NOLA as a kid.

Laura works closely with the MML culinary team to spitball menu ideas and come up with new dishes. Flounder piccata offers a light alternative to veal, and features local seafood. The fresh linguine vongole combines homemade pasta topped with a toasted garlic butter sauce studded with Manila clams, a plump, juicy variety that brings wow to the dish.

The menu is seafood-centric, with an emphasis on seasonal, sustainably line-caught and bycatch fish. Oysters are available raw or grilled with Parmesan butter. But steak lovers won't be disappointed by the bistecca alla Fiorentina, a twenty-four-ounce dry-aged porterhouse from Meats by Linz of Chicago. Grilled over oak and, served with brown butter and garlic confit, this dish would be at home at any of the meat palaces in Florence. Have a drink at the sexy Paradise Lounge before or after dinner. And dress to impress.

Flounder Piccata
See page 246

FLOUNDER PICCATA

This light take on traditional piccata, usually made with veal or chicken, speaks to chef Laura's focus on coastal Italian seafood at San Lorenzo. Made with demi-glace at the restaurant, which imbues a rich, robust flavor to the sauce, this version can work with good-quality chicken stock. Her snapper Française is another menu adaptation to try at this lovely spot in the Garden District.

SERVES 2

FLOUNDER

2 (6-OUNCE) FLOUNDER FILLETS

SALT AND PEPPER, TO TASTE

6 TABLESPOONS ALL-PURPOSE FLOUR

¼ CUP UNSALTED BUTTER

1. Season flounder fillets with salt and pepper. Dredge flounder in flour and set aside.

2. Melt butter in sauté pan over high heat. When butter starts to slightly smoke, add flounder and turn down heat to medium.

3. Cook until bottom of fillets in the pan is golden brown, roughly 2–3 minutes. Flip and cook another 2 minutes on opposite side. Remove fish and set aside.

SAUCE

2 TABLESPOONS CAPERS

¼ CUP VEAL DEMI-GLACE OR GOOD-QUALITY LOW-SODIUM CHICKEN STOCK

½ CUP DRY WHITE WINE

1 TABLESPOON UNSALTED BUTTER

1 TEASPOON FRESH LEMON JUICE, PLUS MORE TO TASTE

SALT AND PEPPER, TO TASTE

1. In same pan used to cook fish, add capers and fry until crispy, 30–45 seconds.

2. Drain any remaining butter from pan. Add demi-glace or stock and white wine and reduce over high heat until sauce has slightly thickened and coats a spoon, about 10 minutes.

3. Lower heat to medium, add butter, and stir into sauce just until melted. Season with lemon juice, and adjust seasoning, if needed, with salt and pepper.

SPINACH

2 TABLESPOONS EXTRA-VIRGIN OLIVE OIL

4 CUPS PACKED SPINACH

1 TABLESPOON FRESH LEMON JUICE

SALT AND PEPPER, TO TASTE

1. In separate pan, heat olive oil. Add spinach and lemon juice.

2. Sauté spinach until just wilted. Season with salt and pepper to taste.

To Serve

1. Add spinach to each plate and top with flounder fillet.

2. Pour sauce around fish. Enjoy!

SEAFOOD SALLY'S

8400 Oak Street

A GLOBE-TROTTING CHEF EXPANDS THE NOLA TABLE

Marcus Jacobs is a traveler. His wanderlust informs his cooking and what's for dinner at Marjie's Grill and Seafood Sally's, the two restaurants he owns with his partner and fellow traveler, Caitlin Carney.

The Ohio native's career started, like that of so many chefs, as a dishwasher at a white-tablecloth joint. When a pantry cook didn't show up, the chef gave him a shot. His trajectory has been skyward since, working with Alana Shock in Columbus, Ohio, then in San Francisco for the late chef Judy Rodgers at Zuni Café.

While in the Bay Area, he lived in the oldest Chinatown in North America. Fascinated by

Chinese, Thai, Vietnamese, and Japanese cultures, Marcus's perspective was expanded, and a job became a vocation.

He spent three months in Japan, working on farms and in restaurants. The experience cemented his passion for quality exotic ingredients and local foods. After seven years with the Link Restaurant Group, Marcus left for an inspirational three-month trip with Caitlin across Southeast Asia. The couple opened their first restaurant in 2017, Marjie's Grill, named for Caitlin's mom. The Mid-City restaurant's South-meets–Southeast Asia menu brought lemongrass, chiles, fish sauce, and Thai basil to locally sourced produce, meat, and seafood.

In May 2021, the duo opened Seafood Sally's, named for Marcus's grandmother, a casual modern Louisiana seafood restaurant Uptown on Oak Street. The idea is to have a welcoming neighborhood spot that serves pristine seafood—a-come-as-you-are kind of place.

There's a raw bar, with Louisiana oysters fresh shucked on ice with nuoc cham mignonette, cocktail sauce, and horseradish. Cornmeal-crusted Gulf shrimp, sourced from Larry "Mr. Shrimp" Thompson, are fried with jalapeños for extra zing. Shrimp and crabs are boiled to order, with blue crabs for picking when they're in season. For the boiled seafood, a coating of chili butter riffs on the popular Viet Cajun style of boiled seafood. There's a grilled fish of the day, caramelized with garlic chili mayo, and an old-school étouffée in a rich crawfish gravy.

Beyond seafood, hot fried turkey necks are tossed with fish sauce, lime, herbs, and honey. There's a yardbird and andouille gumbo and a double patty burger with house pickles, American cheese, and potato wedges.

Sally's, which Caitlin calls their "Pensacola paradise," radiates a shabby-chic beach vibe. All that's missing is the sand between your toes. An inviting wraparound porch and patio are set up for outside dining; inside is a bar, rattan furniture, seafoam walls, and scattered bistro tables.

The community-minded couple sees Seafood Sally's as more than just a restaurant. They want to be a part of supporting the seafood industry in South Louisiana, said chef Marcus.. "Seafood plays a big part of the culture here, and we want to keep that tradition going."

C hef Marcus's commitment to freshness and flavor diversity fuels a pow-erfully good seafood gumbo, simmered in a rich shellfish gravy. Chicken broth can be substituted, but saving shrimp shells and making stock is the best way to go. A store-bought Cajun seasoning spice mix can take the place of homemade.

SERVES 6-8

ROUX

1½ CUPS PEANUT OR VEGETABLE OIL	1 CUP DICED CELERY
1½ CUPS ALL-PURPOSE FLOUR	1 CUP DICED BELL PEPPER
4 CUPS DICED ONIONS	2 TABLESPOONS MINCED GARLIC
½ TABLESPOON SALT	2 TABLESPOONS CAJUN SPICE (SEE RECIPE, RIGHT)

1. Heat oil over medium-high heat in heavy-bottomed pan.

2. Add flour and whisk constantly until roux is dark brown, about 20 minutes.

3. Add onions and salt; cook over medium-low heat about 20 minutes, stirring constantly.

4. Add celery and bell pepper; cook over medium-low heat about 20 minutes, stirring constantly to avoid sticking.

5. Add garlic and Cajun Spice; cook about 5 minutes.

CAJUN SPICE

YIELDS ¾ CUP

2 TABLESPOONS CAYENNE

¼ CUP PAPRIKA

2 TABLESPOONS CHILI POWDER

¼ CUP BLACK PEPPER

1 TABLESPOON GARLIC POWDER

¾ TABLESPOON MSG

1. Combine all ingredients in bowl and set aside.

continued...

SEAFOOD GUMBO

3 QUARTS SHELLFISH OR CHICKEN STOCK, PLUS MORE AS NEEDED

1 BATCH ROUX (PAGE 250)

½ POUND ANDOUILLE SAUSAGE, CASING REMOVED AND LARGE DICED

1½ POUNDS CRAB BODIES, HALVED AND CLEANED

2 BAY LEAVES

SALT, TO TASTE

2 CUPS OKRA, SLICED ¼ INCH THICK

2 CUPS SHRIMP, PEELED AND DEVEINED

HOT SAUCE, TO TASTE

CAJUN SPICE, TO TASTE (PAGE 251)

1. Bring 2 quarts stock to boil in heavy-bottomed pot.

2. Whisk in Roux and bring back to boil, stirring constantly to avoid sticking. Turn down to simmer.

3. Add andouille and simmer for 1 hour; skim any fat that comes off top.

4. Add crab bodies and bay leaves; simmer another hour, skimming fat as needed.

5. Taste gumbo; if there's some bitter notes or it feels too thick, add more stock 1 cup at a time; add salt as needed, to balance the flavor of the Roux.

6. Once gumbo is tasting good, sear okra on stove in separate pan until browned all over, stirring occasionally.

7. Add browned okra and shrimp to gumbo. Simmer 10–15 minutes until both are cooked.

8. Season to taste with hot sauce, salt, and Cajun Spice. Always have someone else taste the gumbo to be sure everything is just right.

THAI D-JING

93 Fifth Street
thaidjing.com

AUTHENTIC THAI FOOD ACROSS THE MISSISSIPPI

Travel along gritty Fifth Street in Gretna, Louisiana, and there's not much to see. Until you get to the bright-pink cottage where you absolutely must hang a right into the tidy parking lot. Here, at Thai D-Jing restaurant, Jeerasak Boonlert and his wife, chef Suda Oun-in, are making savory magic against the backdrop of their hard-won American dream.

Both originally hail from the north of Thailand. Jeerasak arrived in New Orleans in 2008 as a practicing Buddhist monk on a mission, to help build the Chua Bo De temple on the West Bank. Unlike the Catholic priesthood, monks serve a period of time and then can return to laymen's status. He did that, after meeting his wife-to-be at the temple in 2011.

Suda, a classically trained chef certified in traditional Thai cuisine, had transferred from working at a Marriott on the Thai island of Similan to the Marriott kitchen on Canal Street in 2010. "I wanted to see America," said the chef, her face breaking into a brilliant smile. The couple married in 2012, with the goal always being to run their own business. Jeerasak, also an accomplished cook, worked in several Thai restaurant kitchens, including the now-shuttered La Thai Uptown.

What started as a Gretna Farmer's Market concession stand—with the couple offering the likes of fresh pad Thai and chiang mai noodles out of Crock-Pots—grew into taking their business on the road. After two years, they had saved enough money to buy a refurbished 1993 Chevy P30, and in August 2015, they fed folks between Lulling, Abita Springs, Westwego, and Gretna, and, in New Orleans, in Louis Armstrong Park and on Tulane Avenue, close to the hospitals.

They opened Thai D-Jing in August 2020, after working through months of pandemic delays. A few popular menu items include chicken wings stuffed with a savory blend of ground pork, glass noodles, fresh herbs, and grated vegetables, and Suda's award-winning curried soup, which earned the Golden Ladle trophy at the Gretna Farmer's Market competition.

Traditional pad Thai is a crowd-pleaser, with its quick-fried noodles bright with the tang of tamarind and fish sauce. Her ginger salmon is served with a tableside pour of fresh ginger broth. Suda's homemade desserts include an addictive coconut ice cream. The bar serves traditional and tropical cocktails, along with wine and, of course, imported Thai beer.

The couple has settled happily in New Orleans, drawn to its diverse mix of people, including a strong Vietnamese community. "We love this place because it's open to everyone," said chef Suda. "It feels comfortable to us."

PAD KRA PAO NUAR OR THAI HOLY BASIL STIR-FRIED WITH BEEF

This dish is a favorite in chef Suda's native Thailand—simple but so delicious. Although you can make it with Thai basil, Suda prefers the slightly more peppery flavor of Thai holy basil, with its larger, oval-shaped leaves. She grows her own in the garden next to the sunny pink restaurant she runs with her husband, Jeerasak. Choose any kind of protein you like; ground turkey, chicken, or pork all work well.

SERVES 2

4 GARLIC CLOVES

4–6 THAI CHILES, DEPENDING ON LEVEL OF SPICE YOU WANT

¼ CUP VEGETABLE OIL

¾ POUND GROUND BEEF

2 TABLESPOONS FISH SAUCE

2 TABLESPOONS SOY SAUCE

2 TABLESPOONS OYSTER SAUCE

1 CUP THAI HOLY BASIL LEAVES, STEMS REMOVED

4 MAKRUT LIME LEAVES, CHOPPED

STEAMED JASMINE RICE, FOR SERVING

2 FRIED EGGS, FOR TOPPPING (OPTIONAL)

1. Chop garlic and chiles together to medium dice. Be careful about touching Thai chiles, as their oil will stay on skin and burn.

2. Heat oil in pan over medium heat. Fry garlic and chiles until fragrant and light golden in color.

3. Add beef, stirring, then season with fish sauce, soy sauce, and oyster sauce. Break meat into smaller and smaller pieces until cooked through.

4. Add Thai holy basil leaves and chopped lime leaves and stir for a few minutes until just wilted.

5. On each plate, serve on bed of steamed jasmine rice with fried egg on top, if using.

FOUR MORE RESTAURANTS OWNED BY THAI WOMEN CHEFS

New Orleans is an epic food city, but it is not known as a mecca of Thai cuisine. Which is why the opening of five Thai restaurants owned and run by Thai-born women chefs in two years is a big deal. Thai D-Jing is one. Here are four more to try.

BUDSI'S AUTHENTIC THAI, MARIGNY

Chef Budsaba Mason and her husband, Jared Mason, opened Budsi's in December 2021. Try the Isan regional specialty waterfall pork: marinated grilled pork sautéed with onions, cilantro, scallions, mint, and lime juice over jasmine rice.

POMELO, UPTOWN

Chef Aom Srisuk and her husband, Frankie Weinberg, opened Pomelo in November 2021. Order chicken thighs simmered in a massaman curry studded with potatoes, onion, and peanuts, fragrant with cardamom and a hint of star anise. The couple opened a second restaurant in early 2024, the seafood-centric Good Catch in the CBD.

THAI'D UP NOLA, GENTILLY

Saowanit "Kate" Welch and her partner, Ryan Walsh, opened Thai'd Up NOLA in July 2022. Try her Thai'd Up grill: marinated chicken or pork served with a bold house-made jaew dipping sauce that features shallots, fish sauce, chiles, and herbs.

THAIHEY NOLA, FRENCH QUARTER

Chef Orawin "Nim" Yimchalam Greene (pictured on the right) and her husband, Nathan Greene, opened Thaihey in 2022. Get the coconut green curry served with grilled eggplant, Louisiana crawfish, and cheese tortellini, with flash-fried Thai basil on top.

TONTI'S FRENCH BISTRO

323 Verret Street
tontishand.com

AN APPROACHABLE GALLIC RESTAURANT IN ALGIERS POINT

Tonti's French Bistro is the neighborhood restaurant Algiers Point has been waiting for. Situated next to Confetti Park, an important greenspace and a hub for families, in the second oldest neighborhood in New Orleans, the fetching restaurant opened in late 2022.

A collaboration between several local film industry veterans, the restaurant is situated on leafy Verret Street. It's within walking distance of the Algiers Ferry Terminal, where passengers disembark from the five-minute trip from the foot of Canal Street across the

Mississippi to the second most historic neighborhood in the city. Dig in like a local and order a Confetti Park cocktail, and $1 is donated to the park. Made with white rum, Peche de Vigne, citrus, and sparkling brut, a riff on a French 75, the drink is served in a glass rimmed with locally made lavender sugar.

Chef Freddy Augustin commands the kitchen. The central Florida native has spent the past eleven years in NOLA at Café Atchafalaya and as a private chef for a few locals in the film industry. One of his clients, an investor in the restaurant, tapped him for the top chef job. In kitchens since he was fifteen, Freddy isn't formally trained, although he considers Jacques Pépin and Julia Child to be his mentors. "I learned from their words, doing what they did on TV," said the chef.

Freddy isn't overstating his commitment to classic bistro fare. Take the onion soup, for example. The chef spends three days making what is arguably the best version of this classic French dish on either side of the river. Roasted beef bones simmer for two days to develop a stock with layers of rich flavor notes. Two kinds of onions slowly caramelize into just the right balance of sweetness over five hours. It all comes together with butter and dry sherry, crowned with a toasted slice of baguette and an excellent oozing Gruyère.

The menu runs to the classics including escargot Bourgogne, croque madame, trout meunière almondine, and the two-patty L'smash burger finished with cheese and a slather of duck fat aioli. The bistro is named for French general Henri de Tonti, who is also immortalized in a street that runs from the Industrial Canal in the Upper Ninth Ward to Poydras Street by the Super Dome.

For non-locals dining at Tonti's, the obscure general will immediately become a hallowed figure. Thanks to chef Freddy's French onion soup and a menu of charming French fare, Tonti is now firmly etched on the map in Old Algiers.

SALAD BRUXELLES

Brussels sprouts are named after the city in Belgium where it is believed the vegetables were first widely cultivated in the sixteenth century. Brussels sprouts are having a moment: no longer overcooked and maligned, they are instead prized for their natural, nutty sweetness. Light and delicious, this salad is easy to prepare and is loaded with crunch, color, and texture. Salad Bruxelles is also an absolutely perfect way to introduce Brussels sprouts to skeptical naysayers.

SERVES 4

1 POUND BRUSSELS SPROUTS OR 2 (9-OUNCE) CONTAINERS SPROUTS, TRIMMED AND SLICED THIN

4 RED RADISHES, SLICED PAPER-THIN

1 WATERMELON OR HEIRLOOM RADISH, SLICED PAPER-THIN

¼ CUP DRIED CURRANTS, OR ANY DRIED FRUIT OF YOUR CHOICE

¼ CUP SLICED ALMONDS, TOASTED

SALT AND PEPPER, TO TASTE

1 CUP CHAMPAGNE VINAIGRETTE (RECIPE BELOW), FOR SERVING

1. Combine all ingredients, except Champagne Vinaigrette, in large bowl and mix to combine.

2. Chill at least 30 minutes. Serve cold with Champagne Vinaigrette.

CHAMPAGNE VINAIGRETTE

½ CUP CHAMPAGNE VINEGAR

8 GARLIC CLOVES

3 TABLESPOONS STEEN'S CANE SYRUP OR HONEY

2 TABLESPOONS DIJON MUSTARD

1 TABLESPOON FRESH LEMON JUICE

1 CUP OLIVE OIL

SALT AND PEPPER, TO TASTE

1. Combine all ingredients, except olive oil, salt, and pepper, in blender and puree on high until garlic is pureed.

2. With blender on medium speed, very slowly add olive oil until emulsified. Add salt and pepper to taste.

TOUPS' MEATERY

845 N. Carrollton Avenue
toupsmeatery.com

A CAJUN CHEF STAYS TRUE TO HIS FAMILY ROOTS

Chef Isaac Toups is DNA Cajun—as he likes to say, "born and braised." He's loud and proud of it, and loves to party and cook the kind of food he loves to eat.

He grew up in the heart of Cajun country in Rayne, Louisiana, about twenty miles west of Lafayette. More than three hundred years ago, his family left France for Acadia, a region that now encompasses New Brunswick, parts of Quebec, Nova Scotia, Prince Edward

Island, and Maine. Chased from their homes by the British in the eighteenth century, the Acadians found refuge in South Louisiana, a land of bayous for fishing and cypress forests for hunting game. Rustic Cajun cuisine evolved in this rural setting, a style of cooking that Isaac passionately advocates.

The chef comes from a large family that, as he said, "lives to eat." Hunting and fishing provided the main ingredients for seasonally focused celebrations with family and friends. Shrimp and crawfish boils, fish fries, boucheries, and backyard barbecues—this kind of communal eating continues to inspire his modern approach to the cuisine.

Isaac went from cooking in a small-town restaurant to moving to New Orleans, where his wife, Amanda, is from. He honed his fine dining skills for a decade in Emeril Lagasse's restaurant kitchens. He opened Toups' Meatery with his wife in 2012.

Portraits of both his grandmothers hang in the Mid-City neighborhood restaurant. He grew up in the kitchen in a family where everybody cooked. He credits his grandmothers for inspiring him to turn cooking into a vocation. Their influence continues in dishes like barbecue Mississippi rabbit, crispy turkey necks, and mustard-crusted rack of elk.

A magnetic personality in front of the camera and off, Isaac was a finalist and fan favorite on season 13 of Bravo TV's *Top Chef*. In 2018, the four-time James Beard Award finalist wrote *Chasing the Gator: Isaac Toups and the New Cajun Cooking*. "He shares his recipes so casually, it's as if he were telling you how to make duck gumbo over beers in a hunting blind," said *The New York Times*. Isaac is the real deal, which is why his food is so mesmerizing.

The restaurant's Meatery Board is one menu highlight, a hearty selection of house-cured meats and accompaniments. Slow-cooked lamb neck and confit chicken thighs with chicken liver and cornbread dressing are a few dishes that illustrate the chef's sophisticated approach to his culinary roots.

"All I have ever wanted to do is to offer my version of Cajun cuisine and to re-create the dining experience around my family's table," said the chef. Pay a visit to Toups' Meatery and it's apparent—he's nailed it.

DIRTY RICE

irty rice is as common at the Cajun table as mashed potatoes and gravy anywhere else. It's the meatiest, richest rice dish you'll ever eat, and it gets its color, its dirtiness, from glorious sirloin. The trick to this dish is getting a good char on the ground beef. Chef Isaac likes to sear it as he would a steak, before the meat is broken up and braised. That caramelized meat makes the difference between a good pot of dirty rice and something you'd be embarrassed to serve to a Cajun grandmother. You can swap beef for ground turkey if you like.

SERVES: 4–6

MEAT

1 POUND LEAN GROUND SIRLOIN

2 TEASPOONS KOSHER SALT

1 TABLESPOON GRAPE-SEED OIL

½ TEASPOON BLACK PEPPER

½ TEASPOON TOASTED GROUND CUMIN

¼ TEASPOON CAYENNE

⅓ CUP AMBER BEER

1. Season block of sirloin just as it comes out of the tray from grocery store, with 1 teaspoon salt on each side.

2. In large skillet, heat oil over medium-high heat until it starts to smoke. Place sirloin block in skillet in one piece and sear until it browns and caramelizes, 3–5 minutes. Then flip and repeat 3–5 minutes longer.

3. Once block of sirloin is well seared, chop it up in pan with metal spatula to sear inside bits.

4. Add black pepper, cumin, and cayenne and stir well. Cook for a minute.

continued...

5. Add beer to deglaze pan and cook 1 minute longer, scraping up any browned bits. Remove from heat and set aside. At this point, you've got a dark roux chili that also makes a killer ragù for an incredible lasagna. Freeze for up to 6 weeks.

DIRTY RICE

¼ CUP GRAPE-SEED OIL

¼ CUP ALL-PURPOSE FLOUR

½ CUP FINELY CHOPPED WHITE ONION

½ CUP FINELY CHOPPED GREEN BELL PEPPER

⅓ CUP FINELY CHOPPED CELERY

4 GARLIC CLOVES, CRUSHED

⅓ CUP AMBER BEER

1 CUP CHICKEN STOCK, PLUS MORE AS NEEDED

MEAT (PAGE 267)

2 CUPS JASMINE RICE OR ANY MEDIUM-GRAIN WHITE RICE, COOKED ACCORDING TO PACKAGE DIRECTIONS

2 TABLESPOONS UNSALTED BUTTER

½ BUNCH SCALLIONS (GREEN TOPS ONLY), CHOPPED

KOSHER SALT, TO TASTE

1. In heavy cast-iron Dutch oven over medium heat, make dark roux with oil and flour, about 20 minutes, stirring constantly.

2. Once roux is color of chocolate, add onion, bell pepper, and celery and stir. Cook 1 minute. Stir in garlic and cook 1 minute longer. Add beer and mix well.

3. In ⅓-cup increments, add stock, stirring well between each addition. Stir frequently but not continuously until you have a well-emulsified gravy, thick enough to coat back of spoon.

4. Once gravy is done, add cooked beef. Add splash of stock to meat pan to deglaze delicious extra bits that stick to the pan, and add them to gravy and meat.

5. Bring meat and gravy mixture back to bare simmer. Cover and cook about an hour or until gravy has no chalky or floury flavor.

6. Add cooked rice, butter, and scallions to meat gravy in pot. Stir over low heat, just to warm it all through. Add salt to taste and serve.

TUJAGUE'S

429 Decatur Street
tujaguesrestaurant.com

A STORIED RESTAURANT STANDS THE TEST OF TIME

The year 2020 was tectonic on every level for New Orleans restaurants. For Tujague's (say "two jacks"), it was epic for a change of address.

In a city of revered culinary traditions, only Antoine's Restaurant, opened in 1840, has a longer history. Tujague's was opened in 1856 by Guillaume Tujague, an immigrant from France who started with a butcher's stand in the French Market. The restaurant moved from 811 Decatur to 823 in 1914, a building that was previously home to Begue's Exchange, the storied place where brunch was first served.

There, with its familiar stand-up bar, Tujague's held steady through two world wars, Prohibition, and a sea change in the city's cultural landscape.

As Tujague's was always open on Thanksgiving and Christmas, generations of families convened here to celebrate. From deal-making politicos to French Quarter bohos, Tujague's attracted an eclectic crowd of regulars. The move from 823 to 429 Decatur was its second migration.

Groundbreaking it was not. Tujague's had a take-it-or-leave-it five-course table d'hôte menu until 2013. Like other iconic Creole restaurants, Tujague's eschewed trends in favor of the traditional flavors of old New Orleans, sticking with old-school dishes like turtle soup, crawfish bisque, and oysters Bienville.

The restaurant's executive chef, Gus Martin, has mixed things up a smidge. The New Orleans native, whose family has Cajun roots, has cooked at Brennan's, Mr. B's Bistro, and Commander's Palace under Paul Prudhomme, later becoming sous chef. He was most recently executive chef of Dickie Brennan & Co.'s family of restaurants.

Chef Gus has preserved tradition while bringing more contemporary flavors to the plate. His roasted mushroom crepes offer a vegetarian starter. There's a braised beet salad, and a pan-seared Maple Leaf Farms duck breast with foie gras mashed potatoes, as well as a citrus dried cherry demi-glace.

Although the original bar was too fragile to move, the current wooden bar includes the original footrail and light fixtures. The bar is a necessary stop. Tujague's is the birthplace of the grasshopper. Equal parts green crème de menthe, white crème de cacao, and heavy cream, a grasshopper is shaken with ice and strained into a chilled champagne flute before being topped with a float of brandy—an after-dinner Southern throwback that oozes retro charm. Philip Guichet first created the minty dreamsicle at Tujague's in 1918.

The neon-green sipper is still a Tujague's signature, a timeless drink that has remained popular for over a century. What better way to drink your dessert than with a revelatory sip at the bar where it was invented? While you're at it, order a whiskey punch. It was invented at Tujague's too.

Mushroom Crepes
See page 274

MUSHROOM CREPES

When chef Gus traveled to Paris, he discovered how crazy he was about creperies. He was also amazed by the sheer number of different ways French cooks utilized crepes. Because of his background in French cooking, Gus thought it would be a great idea to offer a crepe filled with the earthy goodness of seasonal mushrooms and the richness of chèvre in the menu at Tujague's.

SERVES 6

CREPE FILLING

1 POUND GOAT CHEESE

1 POUND CREAM CHEESE

1 TABLESPOON CHOPPED SHALLOTS

½ TABLESPOON CHOPPED GARLIC

1 TEASPOON KOSHER SALT

½ TEASPOON WHITE PEPPER

12 READY-TO-USE SAVORY CREPES

1. Preheat oven to 250°F.

2. Place all ingredients, except the crepes, in stand mixer with paddle or food processor. Blend until smooth, 7–10 minutes.

3. Place in disposable piping bag with small tip on end.

4. Lay out 12 crepes on clean countertop.

5. Pipe out filling across bottom of each crepe; alternatively, spoon filling into middle of crepe.

6. Take bottom of crepe and roll up like cigar.

7. Place on baking sheet lined with parchment paper and bake about 15 minutes.

MUSHROOM TOPPING

¼ POUND CRIMINI MUSHROOMS, SLICED

¼ POUND SHIITAKE MUSHROOMS, JULIENNED

¼ POUND BUTTON MUSHROOMS, SLICED

¼ POUND OYSTER MUSHROOMS, JULIENNED

¼ CUP OLIVE OIL

1 TABLESPOON KOSHER SALT

1 TEASPOON BLACK PEPPER

1 TEASPOON COLMAN'S DRY MUSTARD

¼ CUP RICE VINEGAR

2 TABLESPOONS TRUFFLE OIL

¼ CUP MINCED SHALLOTS

SALT AND PEPPER, TO TASTE

½ CUP BALSAMIC GLAZE, FOR SERVING

CHOPPED CHIVES, FOR GARNISH

1. Preheat oven to 350°F.

2. Place all mushrooms in bowl. Drizzle with olive oil, salt, and pepper.

3. Lay out on sheet pan and roast 10–15 minutes or until mushrooms are tender.

4. Allow mushrooms to cool to room temperature.

5. In bowl, combine dry mustard, rice vinegar, truffle oil, shallots, and salt and pepper to taste. Add mushrooms and toss to coat evenly.

To Serve

1. On plate, drizzle balsamic glaze back and forth.

2. Place 2 warm crepes on top of glaze in center of plate.

3. Top with roasted mushroom topping.

4. Garnish with chives.

CHEF'S CHOICE

SIX TASTING MENUS PUT DINERS IN THE BEST OF HANDS

Tasting menus are nothing new. In fact, Tujague's, the second-oldest restaurant in New Orleans, had a take-it-or-leave-it five-course table d'hôte menu from 1856 until 2013 (more about Tujague's on page 270).

But New Orleans chefs have taken that idea to a new level, folding local ingredients, sustainable seafood, and humanely raised meats into menus that surprise and dazzle.

Sometimes they are able to accommodate dietary issues with advance notice, but for diners with multiple requests, maybe another kind of dining is a better idea. Chef Ana Castro from Lengua Madre puts it this way: "The idea of this tasting menu is to relax and let me take care of you. This is our house, me and my team. We're in charge—just let it happen."

DAKAR NOLA, UPTOWN (PAGE 108)

Seven courses

James Beard Award–nominated chef Serigne Mbaye's impressive seven-course menu puts a modern spin on traditional West African and Senegalese dishes, with local ingredients front and center.

LENGUA MADRE, LOWER GARDEN DISTRICT (PAGE 190)

Five courses

Short-listed for the 2023 James Beard Awards, chef Ana Castro has created a luscious, modern Mexican tasting menu for one of the most romantic dining experiences in town.

MOSQUITO SUPPER CLUB, UPTOWN

Multiple courses

Chef Melissa Martin cooks the seafood-dominant dishes from her coastal hometown of Chauvin, Louisiana (population 2,575), in a double shotgun Uptown. Hospitality at its best.

AUGUST, CBD

Eight courses

Chef Corey Thomas brings his love of Louisiana cuisine to the table with the precision of a French master. Absolutely one of the most elegant dining experiences in New Orleans.

SAINT-GERMAIN, BYWATER

Ten courses

Chefs Blake Aguillard and Trey Smith create inventive French bistro cuisine (see facing page) in a reservation-only twelve-seat dining room, starting the experience in the bar for a truly movable feast.

YAKUZA HOUSE, METAIRIE

Ten to twelve courses

Chef Huy Pham's enticing omakase menu includes a progression of intricately dressed nigiri, along with surprises like Wagyu, uni, and even foie gras.

TURKEY AND THE WOLF

739 Jackson Avenue
turkeyandthewolf.com

CHEF MASON HEREFORD REDEFINES SANDWICHES
AND SO MUCH MORE

What happens when an irreverent chef with fine dining chops opens a sandwich shop? Mason Hereford decided to find out when he opened Turkey and the Wolf in the Irish Channel in 2016. Gleefully creative, unapologetic, and impossible to categorize, the menu is rooted in nostalgia.

Mason re-created a sandwich he had often devoured as a kid in Charlottesville, Virginia, swapping turkey for in-house smoked ham, cheddar, and cranberry sauce from a can.

The flabby bologna sandwich he loathed as a kid gets a revamp with fried homemade bologna from Leighann Smith of Piece of Meat fame, house-made hot mustard, and a fistful of vinegar-flavored chips on thick slices of white bread.

Food & Wine picked Turkey and the Wolf for best restaurant in America in 2017, calling Mason "a cross between Jeff Spicoli from *Fast Times at Ridgemont High* and Willy Wonka." The restaurant is a hodgepodge of retro images, mismatched vintage china, and collectible McDonald's and Disney plastic plates, perfect for serving elevated stoner cuisine that is beyond fun to eat.

The guy doesn't believe in following a rule book, but he does believe in big flavors done well and a team approach to success. It is an outlook that continues to serve him. Mason opened Molly's Rise and Shine in 2018, an all-day breakfast joint that channels the team's take-no-prisoners approach to comfort food, as seen in the deviled egg tostado topped with whipped egg mousse, refried red beans, cilantro, lime, red onion, pickled peppers, and spicy peanut salsa.

There are sweet potato burritos and the grand slam McMuffin, made with pork sage sausage, hash browns, griddled onions, American cheese, and ketchup on a house-made English muffin. The décor is eye-popping 1980s, not in a self-conscious way, but in a "remember this, isn't it funny?" kind of way. Here, like at Turkey and the Wolf, eaters can pay it forward by donating $8 for a meal earmarked for an unhoused member of the community.

With breakfast and lunch tackled, the former chef de cuisine at Coquette sets his sights on dinner. The team opened Hungry Eyes in 2023, a homage to all things '80s, from batched cosmos to "lipstick-smeared martinis," and with nibbles like grilled artichoke hearts on the half shell, topped with smoky morita chile sauce and melted Parmesan. There's a salad meets tostada: a thatch of greens in between nut- and seed-crusted tortillas. A green turmeric curry swims with bites of smoked catfish and squid rings, with flaky roti on the side. Hungry Eyes' 1980s vibe transports diners in a setting of mirrored tiles, alligator skin–stamped barstools, and ironically ugly lamps.

Chef Mason is scrappy squared, with a weird and wacky vision that somehow really works. Where his hot tub time machine is heading next is anybody's guess.

SOFT-SHELL CRAB SANDWICH

It might seem like New Orleans only has two seasons, summer and Saints. But seasonal seafood is huge, from crawfish to oysters and soft-shell crabs. Soft shells are essentially naked crabs, caught after they shed their hard shell and before they form a new one. Chef Mason adores the seasonal crustaceans, usually available fresh in New Orleans from early spring to fall. The season can be unpredictable, making this sandwich all the more joy inducing.

SERVES 4

2 QUARTS VEGETABLE OR CANOLA OIL, FOR DEEP-FRYING

1 CUP FLOUR

½ TEASPOON KOSHER SALT, PLUS MORE AS NEEDED

½ TEASPOON BLACK PEPPER

4 BIG SOFT-SHELL CRABS (5–6 OUNCES EACH) OR 8 SMALLER ONES, CLEANED (FACE, APRON, AND GILLS REMOVED)

6 TABLESPOONS UNSALTED BUTTER, ROOM TEMPERATURE

8 THICK SLICES SOFT WHITE BREAD

MALT VINEGAR TARTAR SAUCE (PAGE 284)

2 CUPS SHRETTUCE—THINLY SLICED ICEBERG LETTUCE

WHITE OR YELLOW ONION, THINLY SLICED

1–2 JALAPEÑOS, THINLY SLICED INTO RINGS

1 JUICY LEMON

OLD BAY SEASONING, FOR SPRINKLING

1. Heat 2 inches oil to 350°F in large, heavy pot over medium-high heat.

2. Line sheet pan with wire rack or paper towels.

3. Stir together flour, salt, and pepper in medium bowl.

continued...

4. One at a time, put crabs in flour mixture and get in there with your hands to make sure they're totally coated, including underneath pointy flaps on top side, where gills used to be. Give each a light shake, then transfer to plate.

5. When oil's ready, fry crabs in batches so they don't crowd oil, flipping once halfway through and adjusting heat to keep oil temperature around 350°F, until crispy and claws and legs are fried in place, 5–7 minutes.

6. When crabs are done, use tongs to move to sheet pan, and immediately and liberally season both sides with salt.

7. Heat large, well-seasoned cast-iron or nonstick skillet or griddle over medium heat.

8. Swipe butter generously on each side of bread slices. Working in batches, cook bread until both sides are golden brown, 1–2 minutes per side, then move to rack or stand up slices so they don't get soggy.

9. Generously swipe Malt Vinegar Tartar Sauce on all 8 slices bread.

10. Pile shrettuce on 4 slices, perch onion and jalapeños on top, and add crabs. Squeeze lemon all over crabs, top with rest of bread, and sprinkle on Old Bay Seasoning to give tops a thin, even layer of fairy dust. Cut in half and eat.

MALT VINEGAR TARTAR SAUCE

YIELDS 1½ CUPS

¼ CUP CHOPPED KOSHER DILL PICKLE (ABOUT ¼ INCH)

1 CUP MAYONNAISE (DUKE'S OR BUST)

¼ CUP MALT VINEGAR

3 TABLESPOONS CHOPPED DILL

1 TEASPOON BLACK PEPPER

½ TEASPOON KOSHER SALT

1. Give chopped pickle a quick pat with paper towel. Put in bowl with rest of ingredients and mix. Sauce will keep in refrigerator for 10 days.

UNION RAMEN

1837 Magazine Street, Suite B
unionramen.com

CHEF NATE NGUYEN FOLLOWS HIS OBSESSION

When longtime friends Nhat "Chef Nate" Nguyen and entrepreneur Jeff Gapultos decided to open a ramen shop together, they took a trip to Japan to attend the Tokyo Ramen Show, the largest ramen festival in the world. While many Japanese dish definitions are ironbound by tradition, ramen is not. Any dish that has ramen noodles in it is ramen, which leaves plenty of room for the chef to get creative.

After a few years of pop-ups, the duo opened Union Ramen in the Lower Garden District in 2020.

Nate came to New Orleans from Vietnam when he was ten years old. His family started a lunch truck and then a café serving Vietnamese cuisine. After working in the family business, the young chef moved to California to go to culinary school.

Although he grew up eating pho, he discovered ramen in California, where he became obsessed with its depth of flavor and versatility. After he came back home to New Orleans, he worked at Meauxbar and Bayona under chef Susan Spicer before running the postage stamp–sized Kin.

While there are a large variety of ramen broths, pork-based tonkotsu style is most common. Union Ramen aims for a cleaner taste, with a menu that centers on chicken broth and plant-based miso broth.

Ramen is at the heart of the restaurant's menu, with deeply flavored chicken broth the foundation for most bowls. The original tori includes roasted pork, bamboo shoots, scallions, garlic, noodles, and an egg. Dirty mazemen—a brothless ramen swabbed with sauce instead of soupy—is a spicy ode to dirty rice, made with ground beef, tasso, and sweet peppers.

A vegetarian miso ramen includes confit oyster mushrooms, roasted tomato, poached egg, and spinach. Diners also can build their own ramen, adding ingredients like blackened chicken, tasso, confit oyster mushrooms, and ground beef, adjusting the heat with homemade spicy chili sauce.

The chef's rotating menu of small plates highlights local ingredients. Beggar's purse dumplings are filled with pimento cheese in a red wine reduction. There's a crawfish and shrimp lumpia, a type of fried spring roll from the Philippines, and lamb lollipops lacquered with miso and Steen's cane syrup. Nate enjoys doing riffs on the traditional, like his take on hamachi kama, fried yellowtail collar. Usually, the dish is served with a citrus-forward ponzu soy-based sauce. Chef Nate ties the dish to Creole cooking by adding a spinach cream that gives the fish extra depth.

There are menu options for vegetarians and vegans, pescatarians, and those following a gluten-free diet. "That's what I love about ramen," said the chef. "There is literally a noodle combination for anybody."

HAMACHI KAMA WITH SPINACH CREAM AND PONZU HERBS

Chef Nate has years of fine dining experience in L.A. and Vegas, and locally at restaurants including Kin, Bayona, and Meauxbar. This accounts for his strong sense of culinary aesthetics, whether he's creating layered flavors in a bowl of ramen or this polished dish of hamachi, delicately flavored yellowtail. Chef Nate uses kombu kelp to bring earthy, herbaceous notes to this stunning combination of fish and spinach cream. The dried kombu is available at any Asian market, or substitute for another dried Japanese seaweed. Chef Nate uses hamachi collars at the restaurant, but using fillets is easier at home.

SERVES 4

SPINACH CREAM

1 TEASPOON NEUTRAL OIL	1 CUP HEAVY CREAM
1 CUP SPINACH	SALT AND PEPPER, TO TASTE

1. In hot medium pan, add oil, then spinach, and sauté until leaves start to release their liquid.

2. Set aside to cool, and squeeze out any liquid.

3. Add heavy cream to spinach in pan over low heat.

4. Once sauce starts to simmer, cook another 5 minutes and remove from heat. Add salt and pepper to taste.

PONZU HERBS

3 TABLESPOONS SOY SAUCE

¾ CUP HOT WATER

16 X 6–INCH PIECE OF DRIED KOMBU OR OTHER SEAWEED

1 CUP BONITO FLAKES

½ SHALLOT

1 GARLIC CLOVE

½ CUP CILANTRO LEAVES

½ CUP MINT LEAVES

½ ROASTED RED PEPPER (JARRED IS FINE)

1 TABLESPOON YUZU JUICE

½ TEASPOON XANTHAN GUM (A THICKENING AGENT AVAILABLE ONLINE AND IN ASIAN GROCERY STORES)

1. In bowl, combine soy sauce, hot water, kombu, and bonito flakes. Soak 30 minutes, then drain through strainer; save liquid.

2. Add everything else to blender with soy sauce liquid and blend until smooth.

HAMACHI KAMA

4 HAMACHI COLLARS OR FILLETS, OR TUNA FILLETS

ALL-PURPOSE FLOUR, FOR DUSTING

ABOUT 1 QUART NEUTRAL OIL

SALT AND PEPPER, TO TASTE

1. Lightly dust hamachi or tuna with flour.

2. Heat 2 inches oil to 375°F in large, heavy pot over medium-high heat.

3. Line sheet pan with wire rack or paper towels.

4. One fillet at a time, deep-fry 7 minutes. Remove cooked fillets to wire rack or paper towels.

5. Season with salt and pepper to taste.

To Serve

1. Smear warm Spinach Cream on plate using ladle, starting from center of plate and moving outward in circular motion.

2. Place Hamachi Kama in center of plate, topped with ¼ cup Ponzu Herbs.

METRIC CONVERSIONS

US Measurement	Approximate Metric Liquid Measurement	Approximate Metric Dry Measurement
1 teaspoon	5 ml	5 g
1 tablespoon or ½ ounce	15 ml	14 g
⅛ cup or 1 ounce	30 ml	29 g
¼ cup or 2 ounces	60 ml	57 g
⅓ cup	80 ml	76 g
½ cup or 4 ounces	120 ml	113 g
⅔ cup	160 ml	151 g
¾ cup or 6 ounces	180 ml	170 g
1 cup or 8 ounces or ½ pint	240 ml	227 g
1½ cups or 12 ounces	350 ml	340 g
2 cups or 16 ounces or 1 pint	475 ml	454 g
3 cups or 1½ pints	700 ml	680 g
4 cups or 2 pints or 1 quart	950 ml	908 g

ABOUT THE AUTHOR

Beth D'Addono is a food and travel writer who is passionate about her home city of New Orleans. She loves writing about the many creatives that power the city's deeply entrenched local culture, especially the cuisine, cocktails, and music that fill these iconic neighborhoods. Besides *City Eats: New Orleans*, she is the author of *100 Things to Do in New Orleans before You Die*, now in its third edition. She is a founding member and past president of the New Orleans chapter of Les Dames d'Escoffier.

She dedicates this book to all of the people who set the table, feed their guests, and practice the ultimate hospitality in New Orleans, no matter what, every single day.

– ABOUT CIDER MILL PRESS BOOK PUBLISHERS –

Good ideas ripen with time. From seed to harvest, Cider Mill Press brings fine reading, information, and entertainment together between the covers of its creatively crafted books. Our Cider Mill bears fruit twice a year, publishing a new crop of titles each spring and fall.

"Where Good Books Are Ready for Press"
501 Nelson Place
Nashville, Tennessee 37214

cidermillpress.com

SCALE IN FEET
One Mile

LAKE PONTC

WEST END

SPANISH FORT

WEST END
LAKE SHORE PARK

GUIDE

1. The Times-Picayune Building.
2. U. S. Postoffice.
3. U. S. Customhouse.
4. City Hall.
5. Civil District Court.
6. Criminal District Court.
7. Central Fire Station.
8. Delgado Art Museum.
9. New Orleans Public Library.
10. Howard Library and Confederate
   Memorial Hall.
11. Union Station (Ill. Central R. R., Sou.
   Pac. R. R., Miss. Valley R. R., Gulf
   Coast Lines).
12. Terminal Station (Southern Railway
   System, N. O. Great Northern R. R.,
   La. Railway & Navigation Co.)
13. Louisville & Nashville R. R. Station.
14. Trans-Mississippi Terminal (Texas &
   Pacific R. R.)
15. Louisiana Southern R. R. Station.
16. N. O. Ft. Jackson & Grand Isle R. R.
   Station.
17. Lee Circle.
18. French Market.
19. Poydras Market.
20. St. Roch Chapel.
21. Heinemann (Baseball) Park.
22. Jackson Square.
23. Lafayette Square.
24. Coliseum Place.
25. Beauregard Square.
26. Annunciation Square.
27. Palmer Park.
28. Washington Square.
29. Taylor Square.
30. Shakespeare Park.
31. Clay Square.
32. Frederick Square.
33. Macarty Square.
34. Lawrence Square.
35. Samuel Square.
36. Desaix Park.
37. Lima Square.

N

CITY PARK

CITY PARK

FAIR
GROUNDS

SOUTHPORT

M